A PLACE FOR BEAUTY
IN THE THERAPEUTIC ENCOUNTER

A PLACE FOR BEAUTY IN THE THERAPEUTIC ENCOUNTER

Dorothy Hamilton

THE HARRIS MELTZER TRUST

Published in 2021 by The Harris Meltzer Trust
60 New Caledonian Wharf
London SE16 7TW

British Library Cataloguing in Publication Data
A C.I.P. for this book is available from the British Library

ISBN 978 1 912567 78 2

Edited, designed and produced by The Bourne Studios
www.bournestudios.co.uk

Printed in Great Britain
www.harris-meltzer-trust.org.uk

CONTENTS

I thank my good friends and colleagues who read the draft of this book and offered invaluable suggestions: Lindsay Wells and Mary Hughes, who read from the professional perspective, and Annette and Edward Tomarken as laypeople. I thank too my friend Rick Stanwood for his patience and wisdom as supervisor while I struggled with a PhD, abandoned as soon as I realised I would prefer to write a book; and my friend Bernard Burgoyne who, at a critically low point in the book's early days, not only told me I should certainly write it, but characteristically got up, went out of the room into a house piled with many thousands of books, and returned with a small volume to show me just how short a book could be these days. I thank also my great neighbour Julia, who staunchly checked through the references. Above all, I thank my beloved sister Margaret for unfailing faith in me, much hard work on the drafts, and for combining the blessing of likemindedness with that of the uninhibited critic: To all these people, and to the many other colleagues, friends, students, supervisees and patients who have influenced me, I owe a big debt of gratitude.

To my alma mater, AGIP (the Association for Group and Individual Psychotherapy) for its continuing faithfulness to our founding traditions of philosophical breadth, inclusiveness and adventurousness.

Dorothy Hamilton is a Professional Member of the Association for Group and Individual Psychotherapy (AGIP), formerly its chair; a member of the College of Psychoanalysts; and Honorary Fellow of the UK Council for Psychotherapy.

In a former career she taught emotionally and behaviourally disturbed children; she was co-founder of PACT (Parents, Children and Teachers), the home learning initiative, co-writing Methuen's *Parent, Teacher, Child* and *Learning at Home*. She took an MA in the Psychology of Religion at Heythrop College, gaining a distinction for her work on mapping the language of psychoanalysis to that of religious experience. She has taught, given papers and published on a wide range of psychotherapeutic subjects, often with a bias toward metapsychology, and in a variety of settings. Amongst these, she ran a series of conferences on 'Psychoanalysis and the Nature of Consciousness', of which many of the papers were published in the *British Journal of Psychotherapy*. Groups she has run include a clinical support group at the Nordoff Robbins Music Therapy Centre and a staff group at Holloway Prison.

Interests beyond professional ones include walking in the countryside, especially in mid-Wales and Northern Greece; and local conservation, playing a part in the protection of the Hampshire chalk streams.

This book is written for all those who work under the broad banner originally unfurled by Freud, and which has since opened over such a wide and diverse field of knowledge and practice. It is also for their patients and clients, and for anyone who loves beauty and wants to think more about its place in the mind.

Throughout, I have used the terms 'psychoanalysis' and 'psychoanalyst' for the work and its practitioners. This is in part for the obvious reason that in such a widespread field a single name is necessary to avoid simply listing or interchanging the possible titles – psychoanalytic psychotherapist, psychodynamic psychotherapist or counsellor, clinical psychologist, and more. The terms I chose can of course be narrowly interpreted, but I believe that in light of Freud's huge philosophical outlook, he would recognise them as belonging generically and semantically to all those who practise along the broad lines he and those who have followed him laid down. Another and self-evident reason for using the terms is that in the main it is those who practise under the title 'psychoanalyst' whose ideas I follow in this book, they having led the field in this distinctive form of exploration of the mind.

In beauty, I walk
With beauty before me, I walk
With beauty behind me, I walk
With beauty above me, I walk
With beauty all around me, I walk
With beauty within me, I walk
It is finished in beauty
It is finished in beauty
It is finished in beauty
It is finished in beauty.

(Song from the Navaho Night Chant Ceremony
Flagstaff Museum, Arizona)

To write about beauty is to address a subject that is at once profound and fragile. This is not an easy combination. I write with a sense of temerity, led not so much by any idea of my own competence to do so, as by a long-felt concern that the concept of beauty is too absent from psychoanalytic thinking. In this book I have set out to explain what I mean in speaking of this absence, to review some of what has actually been written about beauty until now, and to wonder what more there may be to say, and to think about, for the future.

I trace the history of beauty and its aesthetic setting in psychoanalytic thought, using Wilfred Bion as the fulcrum in a 'before and after' scenario, since it was largely he who opened up the aesthetic paradigm, leading to new and generative thinking from others. Chapter 1 begins at the beginning with Freud: his thinking on the subject of beauty may have been limited, but as we should expect, he had some radical things to say. I go on to offer some of my own thoughts on the nature of beauty, in particular its qualities of elusiveness. Chapter 2 addresses some of the first serious recognitions of the significance of beauty in psychoanalysis, and Chapter 3 returns to consider early psychoanalytic thought on the subject, tracing its development prior to the advent of Bion; he and his near-contemporary and proponent Donald Meltzer are the subjects of Chapter 4. In Chapter 5 I review some more recent contributions, especially that of Meg Harris Williams. Chapter 6 is a case study illustrating Meltzer's pivotal concept of aesthetic conflict. In Chapters 7 and 8 I explore the key relationship between beauty and knowing, including a consideration of ugliness, and another of the place of beauty in practice: here may be found the meaning of the Aeolian harp pictured on the book's cover. Also here is a reflection on the near-universal love of beauty in nature. Chapter 9 is a further case study, designed to illustrate another of Meltzer's central ideas, that of the 'beauty of the method'. And I close with an epilogue that visits what may be called the two birthplaces of beauty – those of the prehistoric caves and of the mother-baby encounter.[1]

I do not find it possible to speak of beauty, or certainly our more profound experiences of it, without considering what is meant by truth. Bion, like Keats, understood beauty and truth Platonically, and as being deeply interrelated, if not actually synonymous. Besides his formulation of K and the K-link, signifying the human longing for knowledge, Bion spoke freely of truth as a reality that is perhaps better expressed by calling it Truth. This makes it no easier to define, though Bion does his best for us, supplying a string of words by which attempts have been made to express the inexpressible: 'I shall use the sign O to denote that which is the ultimate reality represented by terms such as ultimate reality, absolute truth, the godhead, the infinite, the thing-in-itself' (1970, p. 26). Bion's Truth then lies beyond what we can consciously apprehend, an 'ultimate reality' in the existence of which we may or may not choose to place our faith. For me, any close consideration of beauty points toward the assumption of such a reality.

Equally, an attempt must be made at the outset to define beauty itself in a book of which it is the subject. This is no easier

---

1 Here as elsewhere the word 'mother' is to be understood as the principal carer(s), without losing any of its emotional charge.

than defining truth, but I offer here some ideas based on the thinking of James Kirwan in his book *Beauty*, which scrutinises the concept in philosophical depth. Before addressing the question of definition, Kirwan considers our common understanding of what is intended by the word 'beauty':

> For what is extraordinary is not that sometimes even apparently antithetical qualities are considered beautiful – that what is ugly here and now was beautiful there and then, and vice versa – but that the connotation of the word 'beautiful' remains stable, that the idea of beauty, this mute concept, has existed both here and there, then and now. (Kirwan, 1999, p. 4)

'Then' may connote a time when beauty was understood to reside in formal qualities in the world outside ourselves; 'now' we speak of the eye of the beholder, by which we mean of course the mind behind the eye. Not that this more recent formulation necessarily tallies with our felt experience. Perhaps the most striking characteristic of beauty as a phenomenon is the way it lies experientially – even uniquely – athwart the realms of the inner and outer worlds. We may 'know' that the event of seeing beauty is one that takes place in our minds; the experience itself however is more likely to be of a quality 'out there', and somehow inhering in the object, attribute or idea. This characteristic itself raises interesting questions that I revisit in the context of beauty and knowing.

What then is the nature of the experience of beauty itself? A typical dictionary definition runs: 'combination of qualities, as shape, proportion, colour, that delights the sight; combined qualities delighting the other senses, the moral senses, or the intellect' (Concise Oxford English Dictionary). Kirwan offers a 'classical' definition based on Kant:

> that quality we attribute to whatever pleases immediately, that is, pleases in itself, irrespective of any concept of, or interest in, the object (material or ideal) to which it is attributed. What is beautiful appears to us as an object of necessary delight, though we remain aware that the grounds of this delight are subjective. (Kirwan, p. 6)

Kirwan himself has more to say about the nature of that delight. He says: 'Beauty is immediately and ... irreducibly a sensation – it strikes me' (p. 6). He further describes it variously as a feeling, an event, an emotion, an idea. In this, he demonstrates the sheer emotional range of the experience of beauty.

For myself, the simple term 'immediate delight' is almost sufficient, and is the nearest I can get to the meaning without finding myself enmeshed in qualifications that only obscure the essential and instant clarity of beauty. Even so, 'immediate delight' is hardly satisfactory. Beauty belongs in the world of qualia: its meaning cannot be conveyed to a (hypothetical) person who has not experienced it. I think we could do with a new word, one that simply means 'response to beauty'.

It is probably already clear that my understanding of beauty in the psychoanalytic context belongs in that dimension of human experience we call the spiritual. This dimension has gained widespread recognition only in the past decade or so, and it may be that the earlier conflation of spiritual experience with religious belief systems has prevented psychoanalysis from giving much serious thought to beauty, which tends to point immediately toward the spiritual. Here I have been much influenced by the thought of the (beautifully-named) theologian Hans Urs von Balthasar, who has made beauty a central field of study, and claims its place as foremost amongst the 'transcendental' elements, or 'absolutes'.

In view of the foregoing, it may seem strange that the thinking of Jung and the Jungians are not included in the book. Rather than attempt to cover too wide a field, I have confined myself to my own discipline of psychoanalysis, and leave it to others more knowledgeable in analytical psychology to write about its contribution to the subject of beauty.

Finally, I should clarify that it is beauty itself, and the apprehension of beauty, with which I am concerned here – as distinct from expressive creativity, about which others in our field have written more extensively. While creativity will certainly play an important part in my theme, it is not where my main emphasis lies. And I should acknowledge here that within that emphasis lies another: namely, the assumption that where beauty is concerned, both writer and reader are likely to find that it is visual beauty that comes first to mind. This bias toward the visual is found in most texts about beauty, and is perhaps particularly unsurprising in the context of psychoanalysis, since for the most part it is the visual faculty that founds unconscious phantasy and symbolism; of these much more will be said in this book. It is though far from my intention that visual beauty should take special precedence over other kinds. Of equal importance are auditory beauty and the beauty of ideas, to name but two: a point that should be particularly borne in mind in the discussion of the relationship betwen vision and symbolism in Chapter 7. Meanwhile, readers are invited to understand the use of the word 'beauty', as intended to represent all forms, and to choose for themselves their interpretation of its meaning.

My hope is to shed some illumination into what has hith-erto been a somewhat shadowy corner of our thinking, and to suggest the value to us of bringing beauty more fully into consciousness in relation to work with our patients.

CHAPTER ONE

Elusive Beauty

Founding thoughts

F reud, surveying the myriad causes of human unhappi-
ness in *Civilization and its Discontents* (1930), under-
takes to draw up a list of the ways in which we seek to
avoid or overcome our suffering. I find this list of interest not
so much because of its contents, which doubtless most of us
could enumerate, but because of the way it is constructed.

Freud begins by asking what humans 'show by their behaviour to be the purpose and intention of their lives', and answers
himself: 'They strive after happiness, they want to become happy
and to remain so' (*SE,* 21, p. 76). Noting that 'there is no possibility at all of [this] being carried through; all the regulations of the
universe run counter to it', he embarks on his list. He looks first
at the ways in which we try to alter external circumstances, but
soon decides that 'In the last analysis, all suffering is nothing else
than sensation; it only exists insofar as as we feel it'. Therefore 'the
most interesting methods of averting suffering are those which
seek to influence our own organism' (p. 78).

He proceeds to a set of categorisations that progress from
'the crudest, but also the most effective of these methods',

namely the chemical one of intoxication (of which he duly acknowledges the downside); through attempts to 'control the instincts'; to the more refined method of artistic sublimation. Then comes the recourse to illusion, deriving from 'the life of the imagination', and descending in short order to delusions, including the mass variety, chief amongst which he classes religion.

At this point Freud pauses. He reflects that he does not believe he has made 'a complete enumeration', and then rather mysteriously tells us there is one procedure he has not yet named. He keeps us in suspense, embarking on a dramatic build-up: 'how could one possibly forget, of all others, this technique of the art of living?' he asks, (p. 81), and dwells at some length on its many merits. By the time he gives us its name, we are expecting something considerable – nor are we disappointed. It is none other than 'the way of life that makes love the centre of everything, which looks for all satisfaction in loving and being loved' (p. 102). Here evidently we have arrived at Freud's best answer to mankind's endeavours to be happy, or at least less unhappy.

But not so. Freud, it turns out, has after all not yet arrived at his final offering. Without preamble, he simply adds another: 'We may go on from here to consider the interesting case in which happiness in life is predominantly sought in the enjoyment of beauty (p. 82). This seems odd, following as it does on what looked so like the final, not to say climactic, item. The propensity to enjoy beauty is given this singular treatment without explanation, though till now the logic of his various arguments has been characteristically painstaking. It is as though he were singling it out as being of a different order from the rest; and so indeed, from what he goes on to say about it, he believes it is.

He fleshes out his 'interesting case': this is found 'wherever beauty presents itself to our senses and our judgement – the beauty of human forms and gestures, of natural objects and landscapes and of artistic and even scientific creations'. While 'the aesthetic attitude' cannot protect against suffering, yet 'it can compensate for a great deal'. Its enjoyment has a 'peculiar, mildly intoxicating quality of feeling'. It has 'no obvious use; nor is there any clear cultural necessity for it. Yet civilization 'could not do without it' (p. 82). Freud appears to be struggling to explain something hard to understand, a main characteristic of which is paradox. It is peculiar, intoxicating, apparently unnecessary; it is essential to the civilised world.

Strikingly though, any difficulty Freud found in placing beauty epistemologically is in no way echoed where it is a matter of experiencing it himself. In his paper 'On Transience' 1916), in which he establishes the link between beauty and loss, he tells of 'a summer walk through a smiling countryside' with a companion, understood to be the poet Rilke, who was downcast by the perception that the beauty that surrounded them must fade. Freud protested vigorously:

> It was incomprehensible, I declared, that the thought of the transience of beauty should interfere with our joy in it ... The beauty of the human form and face vanish for ever in the course of our own lives, but their evanescence only lends them a fresh charm. A flower that blossoms only for a single night does not seem to us on that acount less lovely. Nor can I understand any better why the beauty and perfection of a work of art or of an intellectual achievement should lose its worth because of its temporal limitation. (*SE*, 14, p. 305)

A deep love of beauty comes unmistakably through this passage. We can begin to see why it might assume a special place in Freud's list.

Beauty's absence

Yet this quality, so central to civilization, which Freud seems to think of Platonically as an essential good in its own right, is a far from familiar topic in our field. There is little to be found about it in the literature, nor in my experience do we discuss it much amongst ourselves. It is as though it were hardly there for us as having any real significance for our work. Freud himself recognised and regretted this absence:

> The science of aesthetics investigates the conditions under which things are felt as beautiful, but it has been unable to

give any explanation of the nature and origin of the beauty ...
Psychoanalysis, unfortunately, has scarcely anything to say
about beauty either. (*SE*, 21, p. 82)

Perhaps Freud himself is in part to blame, given the place
to which he assigns the origins of the human propensity for
aesthetic appreciation, and the language he uses to deal with
it. In the context of our capacity to respond to the beautiful,
the term 'scopophilic part-instinct' strikes a jarring note. It
sounds perhaps a little better as the original German *Schaulust,*
which conveys at least more of the intensity of the feelings
that can be roused in looking; but overall the concept fails in
adequacy. This if any of Freud's theories invites the charge of
reductionism.

Hanna Segal served the cause n better for the Kleinian
perspective, by preserving almost the same degree of silence on
the subject of beauty as did Klein herself, despite the lengthy
attention she gives to the aesthetic capacity in her famous
paper 'A psychoanalytical approach to aesthetics' (1952). This,
it transpires, is concerned almost entirely with the creative
urge and its reparative motivation from the depressive position; Segal says little of beauty itself, or of our capacity to
apprehend it.

Jung too rarely speaks of beauty directly, though when
he does so it is in strong terms. Asked to name the factors
making for happiness in the human mind, he gives one (of
five) as 'the faculty for perceiving beauty in art and nature'
(1960, *CW,* 18: 1719); and suggests that beauty is 'one of the
most excellent of God's creations'. Like Freud, he attempts
no description of its nature, treating its meaning simply as a
given.

It was memorably suggested by Meira Likierman in her
paper 'The clinical significance of aesthetic experience' (1989)
that the aesthetic capacity has been 'assigned to purgatory' in
psychoanalytic theory, at home 'neither in the underworld of
primitive mental life, nor in the 'higher' realm of civilised functioning' (p. 133). Similarly, James Hillman, in his article 'The
practice of beauty' (1998) contends that beauty has actually
been repressed into the unconscious mind of the profession:

'that factor which is most important but most unrecognized in the world of our psychological culture, could be defined as 'beauty', for that is what is ignored, omitted, absent' (p.71). As it happened, Donald Meltzer had brought out his and Meg Harris Williams' book *The Apprehension of Beauty* (1988) just a year earlier than Likierman's paper. Meltzer however remains the only psychoanalyst to have taken beauty sufficiently seriously to write about it at any length; Likierman's comment is still largely true of the field overall. Perhaps its absence is simply a general effect of our present culture, which for the most part holds beauty in no very high esteem; more optimistically, it may simply be that we understand beauty to be beyond words. Still the question arises, does it matter that this concept is so absent from our thinking? I believe it does. Beauty, as Freud and Jung clearly saw, has a critically important potential for our lives. And beyond psychoanalysis, many of humanity's greatest thinkers have claimed it is more than important: that it is of a truly overarching significance. Plato in his *Symposium* has Diotima say:

> This above all others ... is the region where a man's life should be spent, in the contemplation of absolute beauty ... In that region alone he will be in contact not with a reflection but with the truth. (1952, p. 94)

Keats said simply: 'Beauty is Truth, Truth Beauty'. The fourteenth century Mohammedan mystic Hafez said: 'The essence of life is the expression of beauty'. Dostoevsky, obliquely but unforgettably, claimed that 'beauty will save the world'. Schiller said: 'It is through beauty that we arrive at freedom'. And the theologian Von Balthasar (1989) claims that not only is Beauty indivisible from the transcendentals of Truth and Love, but is 'first among equals' in that it is their herald, the epiphanic sign by which we know them. His disciple Angelo Scola states: 'the epiphany of being, that is, its beauty, is the true breach by which being penetrates into man' (1995, p. 32).

These are only a few of many, but the range of sources they represent is wide: poets, philosophers, writers, theologians and mystics, all giving to beauty a place of the highest possible priority. This must surely be a matter of interest to a profession concerned with meaning in human life.

Beauty's shadow

Nor does the interest of beauty inhere only in the glowing celebration of it as a supreme good. Contrastingly, a more ambivalent response has run through its history. Here is the equally interesting question of beauty's shadow. There has always been a suggestion of the suspect about beauty: can it be trusted? might it in fact deceive? After all, Rilke's deep dissatisfaction with its impermanence led him (on that occasion; he was of course a passionate lover of the beautiful) to reject its value altogether. According to Freud, he felt it 'shorn of its worth by the transience which was its doom' (1915, p.305).

Others have felt the same. Seneca the Younger said: 'Beauty is such a fleeting blossom, how can wisdom rely on its momentary delight?' Yeats said of 'the phantom, Beauty': 'All that's beautiful drifts away, like the waters.' For Burns, it was 'the rainbow's lovely form, evanishing amid the storm.' Nor is transience beauty's only drawback. Plato noted disapprovingly 'the plain man's attraction to the outward show of beauty'– and here he had in mind particularly the human face and form, notorious for their deceptiveness. Hopkins asked: 'To what serves mortal beauty? – dangerous.' Keats' 'full beautiful' Belle Dame sans Merci provides a veritable archetype for dangerous seduction. And Tolstoy noted wryly: 'It is amazing how complete is the delusion that beauty is goodness.'

Much of beauty's felt ambiguity clearly stems from experiences of loss and betrayal at human hands. But another potent source lies in the religious tradition that for so long dominated thought, and is frequently cited as a predecessor of psychoanalysis in its aspect of attempting to understand and address human experience. In our western religious tradition, we see the dilemmas around beauty played out with some intensity. 'Favour is deceitful, and beauty is vain', runs the proverb. This again though clearly refers to human beauty: beyond lay beauty as eternal, the 'glory' of the God of the Old Testament. This tradition lasted long into the era of Christianity, to which Plotinus brought the message of Plato's mystical passion for beauty, translated into Christian thought. The beauty of creation was seen as God-revealing. Among the medieval theoreticians, Dionysius said: 'Any thinking person realises that the appearances of beauty are the signs of invisible loveliness.' Augustine went further, effectively equating God with beauty: 'I have learned to love you late, Beauty at once so ancient and so new!' Beauty was accordingly ranked as one of the 'absolutes', or transcendentals. For Aquinas still, beauty is 'the same as the good', being that aspect of the good apprehended by sight, hearing and intellect.

But this attitude became subject in later centuries to the old suspicions. After all, cannot the devil appear beautiful? The Reformation particularly heralded the demotion of beauty from its place amongst the transcendentals, and for centuries it languished, largely ignored. Only recently has it been restored, in particular by Von Balthasar, who has brought beauty resoundingly back into religious discourse with a weighty series of volumes devoted to his 'theological aesthetics'. He laments beauty's repression at the hands of those such as Luther and Kierkegaard in favour of their undue emphasis on word and concept – these presumably felt less likely to lead mankind astray. A plethora of books has followed from theological writers, rediscovering delight and profound meaning in beauty.

Yet again, beauty has suffered a fall from grace in the field of aesthetics and of the visual arts. The twentieth century saw it dealt a blow still more severe than that delivered by Reformation religion. The advent of Dada, provoked by the savagery of world war and followed by the dominance of conceptual art, produced a climate fervently opposed to the traditional view of beauty, heretofore held to be the very essence of art and the chief aim and purpose of the artist. According to the philosopher of aesthetics Arthur Danto in his book *The Abuse of Beauty: Aesthetics and the Concept of Art* (2003), beauty had occupied that place in part through its close association with goodness, and hence with the failed morality the artists deplored. Here however a baby went out with the bathwater when beauty was effectively expelled from artworks altogether. Not only was it seen as irrelevant, it was actively spurned. As Danto put it, a work of art was 'misperceived if perceived as beautiful' (2003, p. 49). In aesthetics itself, says James Kirwan, the word beauty 'appears only as a rhetorical flourish occasionally made by aestheticians in unguarded moments' (1999, p. 93). Danto has played a considerable part in beauty's subsequent part-redemption in the art world. He believes that, while it was rightly dethroned from its overwhelmingly dominant position, it has its own significant place amongst the other meanings that art has to convey through aesthetic qualities, these ranging from disgust to sublimity.

So much for beauty's place in art. Meanwhile, beauty in nature had by the mid-twentieth century virtually disappeared from the discipline of aesthetics, which by now had devoted itself almost exclusively to art. In his 1966 essay *Contemporary Aesthetics and the Neglect of Natural Beauty*, the philosopher Ronald Hepburn laments this disappearance, which took place in the face of centuries of celebration of nature by the writers and artists who loved its beauty. In the midst of a learned article, Hepburn says disarmingly that such neglect is 'a very bad thing', and goes on to leave us in no doubt as to why he thinks so. His essay was so influential that Carlson and Berleant, in their book *The Aesthetics of Natural Environments* (2004), call it 'groundbreaking', and that it 'almost single-handedly' initiated the establishment of a major new field in the second half of the century, namely that of environmental aesthetics. For Hepburn showed that far from being 'subjective, superficial and even non-aesthetic', the natural world 'facilitates an open, engaging, and creative mode of appreciation' (Carlson & Berleant, 2004, p. 14). He put in place a paradigm that recognises appreciation of nature as being 'as emotionally and as cognitively rich as that of art' (p. 15).

It is clear that despite the darker places into which beauty has been thrust from time to time through the centuries, it has the capacity to survive any attacks made on it. It seems appropriate to end this section with a brief return to Danto. While he acknowledges beauty as only one among other aspects of art, he has this to say of beauty itself: 'Beauty is an option for art and not a necessary condition. But it is not an option for life. It is a necessary condition for life as we would want to live it' (2003, p. 160). And again:

> Beauty is the only one of the aesthetic qualities that is also a value, like truth and goodness. It is not simply among the values we live by, but one of the values that defines what a fully human life means. (Danto, 2003, p. 15)

Here Danto both echoes Freud on beauty as a necessity, and simultaneously reaffirms its essentially ethical value.

Beauty and spirituality

The growing recognition in psychoanalysis of a spiritual dimension to the human psyche – often described in terms of the search for meaning, and with an emphasis on intuitive faculties – allows us to place many phenomena hitherto thought of as 'religious' where they seem naturally to belong. In this context, it is interesting that Freud's term *die Seele* may be seen to encompass spiritual aspects of our nature. Bettelheim, in *Freud and Man's Soul* (1982), deplores the translation of *die Seele* into 'mind' in the English Standard Edition, as seeming both to ignore the spiritual connotations of the German word and to disregard its breadth, suggesting perhaps an emphasis toward cognitive aspects. The word 'psyche' may convey a greater idea of wholeness, and might better have suited the original intention. Certain early Freudians, notably Otto Rank and Hans Sachs, spoke of beauty as an expression of *die Seele* in the context of art: both saw beauty as arising from idealisation, and claimed for it a transcendent function capable of resolving psychic conflict.

While many psychoanalysts may find themselves not much concerned with beauty itself, the two 'transcendentals' with which it is chiefly associated in the religious and philosophical traditions might be said to be the very stuff of our work. Love (understood theologically as the expression of goodness) and truth may be very variously defined, but I think few would deny that these are in some way intrinsic to what we do. Our very profession might be said to rest upon a single deep human attribute: the desire for the truth. To express it epigrammatically, we might say we deal in the desire for truth and the truth about desire. Von Balthasar claims that beauty is effectively indivisible from truth and love through the principle of 'circumincession' whereby one inheres in the other in a way similar to that claimed of the trinity. But we do not need recourse to metaphysics to see that circumincession can be tested in ordinary life. The most obvious example is likely to strike us when we look at the person we are in love with, or at our own baby. It is hard to imagine doing so and *not* seeing them as beautiful. While our judgement may (even simultaneously) tell us that others might see that face and form differently, it is not actually possible, in my experience, to separate the apprehension of beauty from intense love *at the moment of feeling it;* and invariably, this is accompanied by a sense of truth, the feeling of 'this is what it's all about', this is reality.

According to these arguments, beauty is integral to love and desire, and to the search for truth, and must inevitably have its place in the therapeutic encounter. Hopkins' phrase 'self flashes off frame and face' might have been written with our work in mind: it recalls the immediacy with which beauty can catch us in the work with our patients. Meltzer speaks of the 'beauty of the method', whereby patient and analyst come to recognise the beauty of what they are doing together, something most likely to happen in the later stages of the work. It is the sense of fit, of rightness, even of poetry; it recalls Bion's 'becoming O in the therapy'. We know when it is happening.

CHAPTER TWO

Beauty Recognised

Donald Meltzer's contribution

Meltzer's recognition of the highly sophisticated form of the apprehension of beauty implied by his phrase 'the beauty of the method' is underpinned by a considerable body of thinking. This embraces not only the significance of beauty itself, but also of its shadow side, and the conflict thus engendered in the psyche that he calls the 'aesthetic conflict'. Both these major ideas will be explored in later chapters and through my two case studies. Meanwhile, Meltzer's inspiration for them began, he tells us in *The Apprehension of Beauty* (1988), with a clinical observation. Speaking of his more ill patients, and commenting on their inability to differentiate between good and bad, he says:

> As the ubiquity of this defect in the more psychotic portion of the personality more and more pressed itself upon me in clinical experience, the more I also became aware of its con-junction with another serious defect: namely the failure of apprehension of beauty through emotional response to its perception. I noticed that whereas the more healt hy of my patients recognised beauty as a donné, without uncertainty,

through a powerful emotional reaction, the more ill were very dependent upon social cues, formal qualities and intellectual criteria. Often their judgement appeared sound, and in some instances even served as the basis for successful careers where aesthetic judgement was quite central. Nonetheless it was clear that, due to the lack of direct and immediate emotional response, they were deprived both of confidence in their judgement and of sincerity in their interest. (Meltzer & Williams, 1988, p. 1)

From here, Meltzer went on to develop a theory that seeks to capture the part played by beauty in the psyche in a way that seems more fitting to the experience of beauty itself than that achieved by previous psychoanalytical theory. In doing so, he took much of his inspiration from Bion, who not only suggested the importance of the aesthetic perspective to psychic life, ranking the 'aesthetic vertex' with those of the scientific and the religious. but has given us a basis for understanding aesthetic development as a primary and essential component of the human mind from the very beginnings of life.

Characteristically, Bion attempts a first-person description of those beginnings with an imaginative excursion into the life of the foetus. Here is a brief sample:

My earliest experiences were of something touching what I later heard was 'me'. The changes in pressure in the fluid surrounding me varied from what Me called pleasure to what Me called pain. My optic and auditory pits ... received sound and light, dark and silent, not usually increasing beyond nice and nasty. (1991, p. 430)

Nice and nasty. Here is the potential for the early, or perhaps pre-, paranoid-schizoid state to be reframed in the language of the senses, fittingly enough for the life of the baby. The terminology of nice and nasty, pleasing and unpleasing, is surely the most appropriate to describe the ground from which the more familiar good and bad, love and hate, originally spring. In *The Apprehension of Beauty* Meltzer leaps boldly into the territory, unafraid to speak directly of beauty and seemingly, like Freud and Jung, unconcerned with its definition. By 'beauty', he clearly means the aesthetic experience that is the most desired, that Bion's foetus might call 'very, very nice'. Meltzer thus adds to the post-Kleinian scenario one of his most distinctive contributions, with the confident assertion of the baby's early ability to perceive not only gradations of aesthetic experience, but beauty itself. He sets out his theme in a much-quoted passage:

> The ordinary beautiful devoted mother presents to her ordinary beautiful baby a complex object of overwhelming interest, both sensual and infrasensual. Her outward beauty, concentrated as it must be in her breast and her face, complicated in each case by her nipples and her eyes, bombards him with an emotional experience of a passionate quality, the result of his being able to see these objects as 'beautiful'. (1988, p. 22)

Like Bion, Meltzer allows himself an imaginative venture into very early perceptions:

> 'At the end of the passage everything was different, surprising, marvellous – and terrifying … those huge and beautiful creatures, so strong they could lift me with one hand ... But it was the beauty of one that overpowered me …Then she showed me the most beautiful thing in the world … I could die laughing and crying and dreaming of being huge and beloved of her.' (p. 44)

These are typically passionate descriptions of what Meltzer calls the 'aesthetic object', beginning with the breast/mother, that will develop into countless further manifestations of beauty throughout our lives. The more usual psychoanalytic language of the emotion of 'love' is thus intelligibly transformed into the language of beauty. Meltzer speaks of the 'aesthetic reciprocity' between baby and mother in which 'from a deeply animal, instinctual foundation, there arises as a product of imaginative thought a bonding at a symbolic level that has its richest manifestation as aesthetic impact' (p. 64). In this reciprocity we take it for granted that the baby's beauty for the mother lies as much in its qualities of 'baby-ishness', its inner attributes and promise, as in any of its physical attributes. That is, it is to a great extent experienced *imaginatively*. But, Meltzer asks,

> is it not the same with regard to the aesthetic impact of the mother, her breast, her face, her embracing arms as they impinge on the baby? Is it not essentially her mother-liness, the manifestation of her interior qualities, that delivers the blow of awe and wonder? (p. 57)

This, he says, is 'love-at-first-sight' on the part of baby and mother alike.

In this state of loving aesthetic reciprocity, there develops between baby and mother a mutual enjoyment of each other that will, again, perpetuate itself into later worlds – of relationships with others, and of artistic, intellectual and cultural pursuits – in short, everything that, in Winnicott's phrase, 'makes life worth living'.

Meltzer's assertions of the importance of beauty in very early development may seem, as he himself acknowledges, to move well into the realms of the speculative. But the thinking that underlies them is not superficial. Alongside his experiences with his patients, Meltzer imbibed from his deep and scholarly reading of Bion a recognition of something central, a 'new idea' the essence of which he succinctly describes thus: 'In the beginning was the aesthetic object, and the aesthetic object was the breast, and the breast was the world' (1986, p. 204).

Meltzer defends himself against accusations of 'speculation' with the simple comment that all ventures into the baby's inner world must necessarily be speculative, and compares more mundane theories unfavourably with his own. Calling on a major poet for support, he asserts: 'This ordinary beautiful baby does come trailing Wordsworthian clouds of glory in his openness to the apprehension of the world about him' (p.16). He could have made wider claims. The parallels here with mythical, poetic and religious versions of the pristine early human condition are evident. All peoples have their Eden. And Meltzer's views would find their echoes not only amongst these, and amongst innatist philosophers of the

Platonic tradition, but in the convictions of a great many 'ordinary' mothers.

A view from the laboratory

Comparatively recently, Meltzer received a possible source of support from a less likely quarter. It is a common observation that where psychoanalysis leads, psychology tends later to follow (though rarely with acknowledgement of what has been discovered before), and now developmental psychology has made a beginning in the area of early aesthetic appreciation. What follows may be read as a kind of footnote to Meltzer's argument, one no doubt narrow in its application but having a validity of its own. Around 2004, a series of newspaper headlines appeared, proclaiming 'Babies prefer beautiful faces'. These were based on a series of findings from Alan Slater and his team of researchers (Slater et al., 2000). Newborn babies were shown pairs of photographs of women's faces, one woman attractive (as judged by adults – they were in fact fashion models), the other plain. The faces were routinely matched for other variables, especially for smiling or serious facial expression.

The researchers then measured the length of time the babies looked at each face. The results were striking. Fifteen out of sixteen of these newborns spent more time looking at the attractive face, and there was an overall preference for the attractive ones over the others of nearly 66%. Many other studies conducted around that time showed similar findings. These results are clearly significant, especially given that the longer attention period is known to correlate with positive response.

Exactly what this significance indicates is, naturally, a matter for speculation. One area of interest, in view of the fact that these are newborns, concerns the possible light the findings may shed on the question of innate knowledge. Do babies arrive with some inborn representation of the human face (the innate, or 'nativist', position), or instead learn visually at an extraordinary rate after birth? Slater notes several lines of evidence favouring the former, and boldly goes further, as quoted in the *New Scientist*: 'Attractiveness is not in the eye of the beholder, it is innate to a newborn infant' (*New Scientist*, 6 September 2004). One line of thought here lies in the assumption that the models' features are likely to correspond to what is known as the 'prototype face'. This refers to the interesting fact that if several same-gender faces are averaged by computer, the resulting face is always perceived by adults to be attractive. From the nativist point of view, the 'attractiveness effect' may result because the prototype more closely resembles the inner representation with which the baby is born.

The attractive 'prototype' face tends to display regular, symmetrical features, and this brings to mind the 'classical' measures of beauty, judged by criteria such as form, line and symmetry. The new findings thus add an intriguing dimension to the old arguments between beauty 'out there', residing in some way in the qualities of the object, and beauty held to be entirely in the mind, or 'eye', of the subject. The researcher J. H. Langlois, whose own work with two to eight-month-olds preceded that of Slater, comments: 'The results challenge the commonly held assumption that standards of attractiveness are learned through gradual exposure to the current cultural standard of beauty and are merely "in the eye of the beholder"' (Langlois et al, 1987).

One way and another, it does seem possible, if not indeed likely, that these babies are exercising an inborn human capacity to recognise aesthetic qualities of the 'formal' kind. Might there now be a case even for revisiting the classical laws, at least in regard to the human face? This would certainly find an echo in the strong human tendency to attribute beauty to the object, rather than accepting it as purely subjective. Kant acknowledges this tendency in his assertion that judgments of beauty by their nature lay claim to 'universal validity': in finding something beautiful, we are almost bound to feel that everyone else will, or should, find it beautiful too. We confidently expect them to share our pleasure in it, and it takes an intellectual reservation to acknowledge that this may be far from the case.

Not long ago I presented the laboratory findings to an audience of psychotherapists, and they got quite annoyed. '*That's not beauty!*' they said of the fashion models. They protested that formal beauty, if it exists, is anyway not the point – that the baby finds the mother beautiful because of the love she shows, and the baby feels. This brought up with some force the question of what beauty is. The therapists were clearly voicing, in their (our) own language, the 'transcendental' point that love and beauty are indeed indivisible: that while we may *know* with a different part of our minds that our object is not beautiful in others' eyes, love itself must see beauty.

Meltzer would undoubtedly agree. His baby is entranced by the qualities of motherliness, as is the mother by 'babyishness'. Yet even he prefaces that claim with this disavowal: 'Despite the outraged cries of innumerable outraged mothers ringing in my ears, I dare assert that a newborn baby is not, in its formal qualities, beautiful' (1988, p. 57). And in another context: 'it may seem likely that the aesthetic impact of the mother on the baby is largely founded on the sensual apprehension of her formal qualities' (p. 64). Here, the laboratory evidence would agree with him! Clearly Meltzer is comfortable with the notion of formal beauty, and is ready to use it as seems appropriate. It begins to look as though both kinds of beauty are in play here. Meanwhile, few of us would feel in much doubt of the outcome if the same experiment were conducted, perhaps at a slightly later age, in which the actual mother's face were compared with that of the model.

Though questions about these experimental findings have doubtless still to be answered, and I have noted only a few, the evidence does strongly suggest that newborns are capable of responding with aesthetic preferences to the first important landscape of their lives: that of the (probably female) face. Not only that, but there is apparent agreement with adults as to what are pleasing and less pleasing attributes. Slater's work, as noted, was far from an isolated study: though probably the most dramatic, it was only one of a series showing similar results, conducted by different researchers over a number of years. It will no doubt be important that such studies are pursued also in other cultural contexts. But whatever interpretations may eventually be laid on the findings, none would seem to obviate the point that these newborns showed a decided preference for certain aesthetic qualities, and that since these were held in common with adults, we may reasonably call them 'beautiful', or the equivalent.

Meira Likierman's contribution

Returning to our own field, and before going on to review beauty's somewhat scanty psychoanalytic history, I turn to the aforementioned paper by Meira Likierman. 'The clinical significance of aesthetic experience' appeared in the *International Review of Psychoanalysis* only a year after the publication of Meltzer and Harris Williams' *The Apprehension of Beauty To my alma mater, Agip (the Association for Group and Individual Psychotherapy) for its continuing faithfulness to our founding traditions of philosophical breadth, inclusiveness and adventurousness.*. Like that book, Likierman's paper stands out as potentially seminal. In it she takes on both the Freudian and Kleinian positions, pointing out that Segal's formulation is no more attractive, or indeed convincing, than Freud's in terms of its adequacy to explain the *origins* of our apprehension of beauty, though she acknowledges the value of both regarding aspects of later development.

Likierman, like Meltzer, believes that 'in the pre-conceptual world the "good" is experienced aesthetically' (1989, p. 138). And she makes clear at the start that, for her, such aesthetic experience must signify appreciation of beauty itself, since 'knowledge of worldly forms is not possible without an exposure to their attractive or repellent influence on the senses' (p. 134). She puts forward the idea, then seemingly radical, that such experience, however rudimentary, is 'primary and present from birth, and that it does not come into being as a result of psychic growth, but is one of the preconditions for it' (p. 133). It is aesthetic knowledge that enables the infant to create mental representations, and thence a phantasy life through symbolisation. In contrast to Segal's argument, 'the aesthetic does not emerge from the depressive phase but enables it' (p. 148).

Looking deeper, Likierman suggests that the apprehension of beauty has its origins in the 'ideal' component of the paranoid-schizoid position. This component, she believes, has been overly pathologised. Because the split-off and 'too–good-to-be-true' aspects of the ideal are deeply implicated in the use of manic defences, denial and omnipotence, the ideal has become more readily associated with pathologies such as narcissism and perversion than with what Likierman calls 'healthy ideal experience' (p. 139). This, like its negative counterpart, owes its existence to the splitting which isolates goodness from damaging influences; but for Likierman, what is produced here is a *primary* state of unalloyed goodness – and therefore, from the perspective of the baby as an aesthetically-sensitive being, beauty. This state, which is of the greatest intrinsic value, should not to be confused with the pathological defensive idealisation that she sees as a secondary development. The 'primary sublime experience' is 'the earliest aesthetic event in an individual's life' (p. 140). And its beauty is closely associated with value: 'We endow all that we value with an unconscious aesthetic 'halo', so that the 'good' is never conceptualised without accompanying unconscious aesthetic phantasies' (p. 148). Here is the fundamental connection between goodness and beauty that underlies the widely acknowledged interrelationship of aesthetics with ethics.

To underline her distinction between the two kinds of idealisation, Likierman suggests that in speaking of very early development we should abandon the dubiously-associated word 'ideal' in favour of the word 'sublime'. Citing the 'oceanic', illimited babyhood state, she claims that for the baby 'the good is sublime, and the sublimity is absolute and eternal' (p. 142). The word 'sublime' is, of course, one redolent of descriptions of great beauty in many contexts and cultures, generally with strong spiritual connotations. Likierman gives examples from her own clinical work, and from art and poetry, suggesting links between early experience of the sublime and later aesthetic and spiritual experiences.

Likierman tells us that the discoveries she made in writing her paper changed its original 'applied' focus, so that 'Rather than applying psychoanalytic insights to aesthetics, aesthetics is shown to shed light on early infantile experience and extend psychoanalytic theory' (p.133). She gives a telling example arising from Kant's formulation of beauty as that aspect of form free from the 'interest' of function or purpose (a view with which Freud agreed). This 'opens the way to our discovery of the independence of objects from the dictates of our needs, and indicates to us the existence of an objective world … Faced with beauty, man realises that he is not God' (p. 135).

There are implications here for our understanding of infantile omnipotence. If we were unable to invest beauty in a whole good object, we would have no means of valuing it except in utilitarian terms, thereby denying the independent characteristics of its goodness. It is the individual mother's *aesthetic* characteristics that 'represent both her independence and also her uniqueness' (p. 135).

Likierman's deeply thoughtful paper places the baby as an active and aware participant in experiences of beauty and wonder, making her vision one very similar to that of Meltzer.

The Rise of the Aesthetic Perspective: Before Bion

Freud and Klein

There seems to have been little response to Likierman's paper, perhaps surprisingly in view of the radical nature of its claims. Could it have been too much of a challenge to the received (Kleinian) wisdom of the time? In any event, that paper, and Meltzer's book, did not at the time result in beauty's being lifted out of its psychoanalytic 'purgatory'. More recently though, and thanks not least to Meltzer's insights into the potential of Bion's thinking, interest in the aesthetic perspective has considerably increased. As Neil Maizels says in his foreword to Nicky Glover's book *Psychoanalytic Aesthetics: An Introduction to the British School* (2009):

> Just as Freud shocked the establishment with news of unconscious infantile sexuality, and Klein shocked the Freudians with news of infantile unconscious sadism, depression, and reparation, Meltzer and Harris Williams shocked the Kleinians – even the Bionians – with news of a crucial aesthetic sensibility and conflict in the mental life of the infant, arch-

ing back into pre-natal curiosity, and ready to bolt out of the gate at the caesura of birth. (Maizels, 2009, p. xi)

The result has been a number of papers and books – including Glover's own – that while not necessarily addressed to the question of beauty as such, nonetheless seem to hold out the promise of beauty's becoming more present in the way we think and approach our work.

Before turning to these, we should acknowledge those theorists who made earlier contributions to our understanding of the aesthetic dimension. These tended to concentrate either on its instinctual or its expressive and creative aspects. Such work, though rarely mentioning beauty in its own right, does offers the picture of a growing web of ideas in which the notion of beauty might flourish. This chapter sets out to trace some threads within that web, and to discover what may be gleaned from them about beauty itself.

Freud: beauty's instinctual roots

Though Freud's idea of beauty as sublimation of sexual drive may now seem narrowly based, we can with hindsight see a broader picture. Hs recognition of the importance of symbolisation in dreams, for instance, laid the ground from which later aesthetic understanding has grown. The concept of symbol-formation underlies our construing of the aesthetic capacity, of perception and of meaning – that is, the whole domain within which our experience of beauty resides.

And though little of Freud's attention seems to have gone to consideration of the beautiful, apart from that passionate defence of it to Rilke, he perhaps did more for the concept of beauty itself than at first appears. The art critic Donald Kuspit argues that Freud performed an important service for the philosophy of aesthetics in his time, dominated as it then was by the thinking of Kant, with his emphasis on 'disinterested' contemplation. Kuspit quotes from *Civilization and its Discontents*:

All that seems certain is its [beauty's] derivation from the
field of sexual feeling. The love of beauty seems a perfect
example of an impulse inhibited in its aim. 'Beauty' and
'attraction' are originally attributes of the sexual object. (*Artnet Magazine*, 2002)

Reductionist as this may now sound, it provided what was at
that time, says Kuspit, a necessary antidote. He points out that
Kant 'never spoke of the love of beauty'. He believes that Freud
restored to the concept of beauty what Kant had passed over, or
even attempted to deny: 'namely, sensation, the body, and above
all sexual feeling, which Kant ignored altogether. It was taboo
to connect beauty and sexuality, and it is exactly this taboo that
Freud broke, and that makes his aesthetics revolutionary.'

And with the body, Freud brought to prominence also the
importance of emotion in our apprehension of beauty. He says
in 'On transience': 'The value of all this beauty and perfection
is determined only by its significance for our own emotional
lives.' He offers a famous example of his concept of *schaulust*, or
scopophilia, in his biographical venture into the life of Leonardo
da Vinci. Here he speculates on the artist's huge sublimation of
sexual energy into aesthetic and intellectual interests – with,
according to Freud's informed guess, a corresponding deple-
tion of emotional energy where relationships with women were
concerned.

The bridge across the gap between the harshness of 'scopophilic part-instinct' and Freud's lyrical celebration of the beauty
of the countryside in spring is made for me by the Freudian
analyst Leon Wurmser, who gives the scopophilic drive deep
attention in his book *The Mask of Shame* (1981). He speaks of
this drive as 'very archaic', and places it in a profound ontologi-
cal context, as reaching 'far back into phylogeny':

Even beauty, that majestic form linking pereceptual and
expressive drives in the service of both love and destruction,
plays as cardinal a role in animal and even plant morphology
as it does in ours (1981, p. 96).

This broad phylogenic theme of the 'archaic' is echoed in an individual life. Wurmser quotes the psychoanalyst David W. Allen,

who traces scopophilia back to the infant's 'rooting' at the breast: 'The rooting reflex with its fleeting searching associated with pleasure is a forerunner to the conscious pleasures of looking and curiosity ... From early infancy the urge to look is strong' (p. 152).

Here, in the intimate connection between searching and feeding, lies the physical basis for a link between scopophilia and incorporation. The idea of taking in, or 'devouring', with the eyes is a familiar one, and often recurs in descriptions of the beautiful. It is closely associated with the state of fascination, which includes the desire (and the fear) of 'losing oneself' in the object, of becoming merged with it. Wurmser's 'pleasurable merger through looking' (p. 155) forms the basis for experiences not only of beauty but of love, and indeed his main theme is that of loving and lovableness, the desire both to see and be seen in an exchange of love. He says: 'Love resides in the face – in its beauty, in the music of the voice and the warmth of the eye. Love is proved by the face ... proved by seeing and hearing, by being seen and heard' (p. 96).

Here if anywhere is established the powerful link between beauty and emotion. Wurmser, an uncompromising drive-oriented Freudian yet hugely wide in his scope, places our most fundamental instincts where he shows them to belong amidst the flowerings of civilisation – the sciences, the arts, the expressions of spirituality. His beautiful book takes what may seem the somewhat unpromising concept of scopophilia, so often associated with voyeurism and other pathologies, and shows that it contains the seeds of some of humanity's finest experiences.

In this context, Freud himself may be said to have contributed in no small measure to our literary inheritance. If he spoke little of beauty directly, his writing perhaps did it for him. Donald Meltzer says that as Freud 'thrilled to the pursuit of knowledge' in his analysis of dreams:

> Freud was surely now finally in love with the method that was carrying him forward. We see the poet, rather than the neurophysiologist, formulating images of symptoms woven around an incident, as a pearl is formed around a grain of sand, or thoughts weaving themselves round an event like garlands of flowers around a wire. (1978, p. 27)

The Kleinian paradigm

It was Hanna Segal, rather than Klein herself, who gave voice to a distinctively Kleinian perspective on the aesthetic dimension. This however was focused not so much on the apprehension of beauty as on the impulse toward creativity, which Segal understood to arise from the reparative urge to restore the lost object following depressive mourning. In her influential paper 'A psychoanalytic approach to aesthetics' (1952), she cites Proust, who held that an artist is compelled to create by his need to recover his lost past, and so to integrate it with his present life. Such motivation toward aesthetic creativity is clearly associated with our theme, and Segal in the course of her paper does speak of 'aesthetic pleasure proper' – though this she confines narrowly to the appreciation of a work of art. She sees aesthetic pleasure as due to 'an identification of ourselves with the work of art as a whole and with the whole internal world of the artist as represented by his work' (p. 204). She believes that 'this kind of unconscious re-living of the creator's state of mind is the foundation of all aesthetic pleasure'.

If, in pursuit of our wider enquiry, we extrapolate from this idea to beauty other than art, such as that of the human form, or a landscape, it will then be a 'mind', actual or metaphorical, that we seek. This would traditionally have been understood as the mind of God, or the gods. From a post-theist perspective, we may speak of projected aspects of the self, or other-in-self. But whatever the nature of the supposed 'mind', it is of interest to ask what Segal believes is being identified with, or re-lived, to produce aesthetic pleasure. Here she addresses herself to the fundamental aesthetic questions of beauty and ugliness, contending that both are necessary to appreciation of the object. Of the beautiful, she believes the main elements to be 'the whole, the complete, and the rhythmical ... An undisturbed rhythm in a composed whole seems to correspond to the state in which our inner world is at peace' (p. 206). She claims support from the art critic Herbert Read, who speaks of 'the rhythmical, simple arithmetical proportions which correspond to the way we are built and our bodies work'. But these elements of beauty, says Segal, are in themselves insufficient:

Soulless imitations of beauty, 'pretty' creations are also whole and rhythmical; yet they fail to stir and rouse nothing but boredom. Thus classical beauty must have some other not immediately obvious element. (p. 206)

This element, she believes, is ugliness. For its definition, she quotes Rodin, who includes that which is formless, unhealthy, destructive, immoral, and much else besides; in sum, everything 'contrary to regularity – the sign of health' [p. 206]. Segal translates this as the expression of the internal world in the state of depression, and notes that depression is closely associated with death. Both artist and viewer have known the darkness of depression and the fear of death, unconsciously or otherwise, and the viewer's identification with the artist's experience of such 'ugliness' is as necessary to the aesthetic experience as is the element of beauty. She concludes:

Ugliness – destruction – is the expression of the death instinct; beauty – the desire to unite into rhythms and wholes, is that of the life instinct. The achievement of the artist is in giving the fullest expression to the conflict and the union between those two. (p. 207)

The theme of ugliness is revisited in a later context. Meanwhile, I find with Likierman that Segal's valuable contribution to the understanding of certain aspects of creativity is less persuasive where it attempts the description of 'aesthetic pleasure proper'. It may seem as though she has placed the origins of such pleasure in the depressive context to fit Kleinian theory rather than because they convincingly belong there.

Making a place for beauty

Alongside the more 'orthodox' psychoanalytic stream, a new paradigm had begun to emerge in the 1940s and 50s with the work of Donald Winnicott and Marion Milner. Both strongly influenced others of the time, notably Charles Rycroft; and an important body of ideas emerged around the themes of transitional phenomena, illusion, creativity and the continuing significance of primary process – that is, early mental functioning – into adult life. Together with the later contributions of such writers as Christopher Bollas and Kenneth Wright, each of whom have developed this cluster of ideas in their own idiom, it may be said that an aesthetic matrix has been created in which beauty might find a place to dwell.

The Origins of Creativity

Donald Winnicott

Winnicott's formulation of transitional phenomena has been hugely generative, not only for our own profession but in many other fields besides. His transitional space – or 'intermediate zone', or 'third area' – is 'an intermediate area of experiencing, to which inner reality and external life both contribute' (1971, p. 2). It is here that the baby's illusion of a fused state between self and mother is gradually dispersed, but not at the expense of illusion itself, which for Winnicott is a rich and necessary human capacity. In the world of transitional experience, the baby playing with the mother's face in a sensory, exploring mode, each 'mirroring' the other, lies at the beginning of a developing trajectory that culminates in the cultural experience of the adult. Here reside artistic and scientific creativity, religious experience, 'imaginative living', and 'the highly sophisticated adult's enjoyment of living or of beauty ...' (p.106).

Winnicott's very manner of writing, his playful syntax and his delight in paradox, are reflective of his own concept of 'imaginative play', play that occurs entirely within transitional space, and is founded in the aesthetic capacity for illusion. John Turner in 'A brief history of illusion: Milner, Winnicott, Rycroft' (2002) says:

> His prose enacts the creativity that it describes; it is a poetry of illusion, embodying the potency of the potential space. It

generates interest; and interest, we might remember, derives from the Latin interesse, to be amongst. To be interested in the objectivity of the world is to be mixed in with it as a subject. (p. 1078)

This is fertile ground for the paradoxes Winnicott loved, the neither/nor, both/and, me/not-me qualities that produce generative imagery in the mind.

Charles Rycroft

Rycroft was concerned, like Winnicott and Milner, to show the ways in which primary process is intertwined with secondary processes from very early in life. He contributed substantially to our understanding of a continuous interchange between them that enriches our aesthetic and creative lives. He claimed that the primary state of 'illusion' in the former becomes, in the realm of the latter, 'imagination'. In so doing, says Turner, 'he discovered one of the major concerns of his writing career: attempting to integrate the psychoanalytic concept of the unconscious with the Romantic literary concept of the imagination' (2002, p. 1076). Rycroft's fascination with the Romantics – the very disciples of beauty, and moreover later named by Bion 'the first psychoanalysts' – enabled him to use the poets to illustrate 'the way that imagination enriches and suffuses our perception of reality', concludes Turner (p. 1078). Indeed Rycroft's writings are liberally sprinkled with references to these poets. He particularly revels in Coleridge's portrayal of the imagination as that which 'dissolves, diffuses, dissipates, in order to re-create' (1979, p. 38); and again as 'that "intermediate faculty" (Coleridge) which enables its possessors to inhabit a world of "both what they half-create and what perceive" (Wordsworth) to "half-create the wondrous world they see" (Young's *Night Thoughts*)' (1985, p. 145).

In a memorable phrase, Rycroft describes himself as attempting 'to marry Coleridge's theory of the poetic imagination and Freud's concept of the primary processes – without, I hope, doing too much violence to either' (1985, p. 277).

Marion Milner

The worlds of illusion and imagination come to life in Marion Milner's work. Her primary concern was with creativity, and she was herself artistic. Understanding her own aesthetic experiences as taking place within Winnicott's 'intermediate zone', her writings develop the theme of creativity from a fresh perspective: that of the artist herself, and above all of the artist as *perceiver*. She is deeply concerned with the subjectivity of the inner world in interaction with the outer, and her writing is imbued with her own passionate aesthetic responses. In her easy and intimate prose, and in the intensity of her descriptions, beauty is present, a given even, whether or no she names it explicitly. Sometimes she does, as in the moving description of her encounter with the Parthenon. Thus, in her early visits to the Acropolis, though 'determined to stalk this beauty by every means I knew ... I still could only *know* the beauty, I could not feel it in my bones' (1987a, p. 19) ('know' used here, of course, in the sense of Bion's 'knowing about'). But on a later visit: 'I did feel as well as see.' She was facing away from the Parthenon, when she suddenly felt strength rising up through her neck and head 'as if I too were supporting a pressure from above.' Then on turning round, she experienced the thing itself:

> And now too I could feel the joy in the plain Doric capitals, the proportions of the rim, the plain circling bit to the spreading curve that supports the square at the top, the absolute rightness of it (1987a, pp. 19–20)

Far predating Meltzer and Likierman, Milner sought the roots of aesthetic development in primary process, arising from the earliest 'fused' experience of baby with mother. She gave great value to the role of illusion, which she believed to be

> necessary for symbol formation, moments when the me and the not-me do not have to be distinguished. Moments when the inner and outer seem to coincide, needed for restoring broken links, bridges, to the outer world ... As necessary for healthy living as night dreams seem to be – and as playing is (1969, p. 416)

In her deep preoccupation with illusion and imagination, art and creativity, Milner's thinking – always rooted in the experience of baby with mother – seems often to prefigure Meltzer's work on beauty. At the Parthenon, an insistent question came to her: 'Is there any forgiveness here? … Or is it an uncompromising beauty, like the beauty of logic and mathematics, a beauty that stands apart and does not bend to one's need?' (1987a, p. 20). Here evoked is Meltzer's 'ordinary beautiful mother' who does not 'stand apart', but 'bends' to her baby's need. Milner relates this to 'everyday experience in healthy infancy' using as example Wordsworth's claim that as a child he was 'unable to think of external things as having external existence, he communed with all he saw as something not apart from but inherent in his own immaterial nature' (p. 98).

The many such experiences described by Milner, repeatedly brought about by her discovery of 'wide attention', placed her in states she felt to originate in the early 'fused' condition; they strikingly recall mystical writings. In her 1952 paper 'The role of illusion in symbol formation' Milner quotes Berenson's 'aesthetic moment'. Here, for the spectator:

> The picture or building, statue, landscape, or aesthetic actuality is no longer outside himself. The two become one entity; time and space are abolished and the spectator is possessed by one awareness. When he recovers workaday consciousness it is as if he had been initiated into illuminating, exalting, formative mysteries. (Milner, 1987b, p. 97)

She says of the Parthenon: 'in a flashed moment I felt: "This is it, this is eternity".'

Aesthetic formation of the self

Christopher Bollas

In *The Shadow of the Object* (1987), Christopher Bollas gives his own understanding of the 'aesthetic moment'. It is that sought-for, but only fortuitously found, moment that recaptures early 'unthought' states of being. This is the baby's experience of the 'transformational object', to which the later transitional object is heir. It constitutes the early handling by the mother, performed in her own aesthetic idiom; the baby's experience of this mutually-created aesthetic forms his/her sense of self. Recaptured in later life, it causes an 'uncanny' experience of being caught up in something. One finds oneself 'embraced' by an aesthetic object – 'a painting, a poem, an aria or symphony' (p. 16), or 'a poet's reverie with his landscape' (p. 31) – and feels a deep subjective rapport with it, a strange fusion. It is a 'caesura in time when the subject feels held … by the spirit of the object' (p. 31). Just so was Milner caught up in contemplation of the Parthenon. In this trance-like state 'I climbed the huge steps of the Temple itself feeling like a child for whom the stairs at home must have seemed as huge as this' (Milner, 1987a, p. 20).

Such experiences, says Bollas, 'crystallise time into a space where subject and object appear to achieve an intimate rendezvous'. In this they feel 'reciprocally enhancing and mutually informative' (Bollas, 1987, p. 31). The word 'informative' is significant here. Milner, having wondered about the actual proportions of the great building before her (Bion's 'knowing about'), says: 'But I did not know. Instead, I plunged into a different kind of knowing'. This 'knowing' is one intimately connected with the deeper experiences of beauty; it will be considered at more length in a later chapter.

Kenneth Wright

Kenneth Wright's book *Vision and Separation: Between Mother and Baby* (1991), does not name beauty, but again depicts a scenario in which beauty is evoked both by his ideas and by his prose. He speaks of the excitement felt in seeing and being seen, its sense of significance and meaning – attributing this not so much to the classical psychoanalytical explanation of sexual excitement as to the excitement of *self-forming*. Canvassing the familiar ground of the infant's move from a state of experienced fusion to one of gradual separation, Wright states this less familiarly in terms of sensory experience, the former state being mediated largely through touch, the latter through vision.

Separation creates a space across which mother and child look at one another. Through the exchange of the gaze and the smile, says Wright, 'I become aware of my self through seeing and being seen – in the "*inter-face*" between persons' (p. 2).

With these words, Wright seeks 'to put the human face back into psychoanalytic theory'. Here, he says, is 'a conversation without words, a smiling between faces, at the heart of human development' (p. 11). Noting that feeding infants tend to gaze at the mother's face, he suggests that this becomes 'the visual aspect of this experience of satisfaction' (p. 13), and thence the image of the good internal object, a core aspect of the self. 'I like to think', he says, 'that the mother's face gets into the baby's experience, not only as the cherished centre of his world, but simultaneously as the guiding light of his mind' (p. 12). The metaphor of light, traditionally associated with beauty in spiritual experience, is much in evidence in Wright's thinking. He suggests that the mother's face 'shines' upon the baby 'and fills its whole perceptual world with its "light"' (p. 19). He does not hesitate to quote biblical texts as expressive of his meaning: 'The Lord make his face shine upon thee … the Lord lift up his countenance upon thee, and give thee peace.'

The Rise of the Aesthetic Perspective: Bion and Beyond (1)

Bion

In tracing the growing tendency to place value and significance on the aesthetic aspects of development, we find a parallel growth of recognitions in a related area of experience, one clearly implicated in the apprehension of beauty. This we would be readier now to call 'spiritual' than would have been some of those who gave us the original aesthetic concepts. Words introduced by writers in the previous section – 'transitional' and 'transformational', 'illusion' and 'imagination', 'meaning' and 'guiding light of the mind' –together suggest a realm of experiencing that at its most intense recalls religious or even mystical states. Coming now to Bion, who may be said to have established the central importance of the aesthetic dimension beyond doubt, we find him also the most 'mystical' of the major psychoanalytic thinkers to date, to the point of his later writings having been disavowed as a serious expression of psychoanalysis by some in the field.

A hallmark of Bion's writing is his assumption of the centrality to human life of what he is not afraid to call 'truth', a word till then not very commonly found in the psychoanalytic lexicon. Speaking of his 'vertices', those perspectives by which we seek to construe experience, he says:

> It would seem absurd if the tension between these three groups – science, religion and art – which are all fundamentally devoted to the truth, was either so slack or so tense that it was unable to further the aim of truth (1974, 1: 95–96).

Here the ranking of 'art', signifying the aesthetic dimension, alongside only the two other great perspectives, tells us the importance Bion accorded it. And the 'truth' to which these vertices are devoted, and are to further, is not to be defined in terms of knowledge, or any other faculty that lies within the bounds of human apprehension. It is whatever we understand by the term 'ultimate truth' which as we have seen Bion called 'ultimate reality, absolute truth, the godhead, the infinite, the thing-in-itself', by way of helping us to grasp his meaning.

Having acknowledged the aesthetic vertex as holding so exalted a position, we may now consider how it is, so to speak, earthed. It is the deep biological basis in 'sensory realisations', the 'nice and nasty' described in Bion's imagined womb experience, that place aesthetic experience at the heart of our mental life. The infant-breast relationship is the prototype for the vital capacity to make the Bionic links that enable mental development – this through 'the embryonic thought which forms a link between sense impressions and consciousness' (1967, p. 107).These beginnings take place within Bion's maternal 'reverie', that deep state of communication between mother and baby that Meltzer takes to be the birthplace of the apprehension of beauty. Here too many other of our themes may be seen to find a home. Milner's 'illusion', Winnicott's 'mirroring' and 'transitional space', Bollas's 'transformational object', Wright's 'interface' – all inhere in Bion's 'reverie'.

Bion has scrutinised, and speculated on, what may transpire in this space more minutely than any before him. In particular, his enlargement of the concept of projective identification, showing its capacity not only to attempt control but, critically, to communicate, has been transformative. Nicky Glover claims that communicative projective identification, among its many characteristics, enables the capacity for empathic and imaginative identification – arguably essential aspects of artistic activity and the aesthetic encounter.

Given the central place to which Bion allocates the aesthetic vertex, direct references in his writings to its theoretical importance are surprisingly few – reflecting again the general omission of beauty as a subject. As a result, the aesthetic dimension is given little attention by the many who have written about Bion, and reference to aesthetic themes is virtually absent from their texts and dictionaries. It is Donald Meltzer, and the scholar and artist Meg Harris Williams, who have been largely responsible for recognising the importance of the aesthetic vertex in Bion's thought, and for developing it in their own very considerable bodies of work.

Yet Bion's readership is left in no doubt of his attitude toward art, the artist, and aesthetic appreciation and expression. This he conveys in his own way, through his love of metaphor and his frequent allusions to poetry, painting, sculpture and literature, and to instances of natural beauty. For this reason, much of this chapter will consist in direct quotations rather than description, in the hope of giving a flavour of the imagery and allusion that transmit his meanings in ways both vivid and profound. Vermeer's little street in Delft 'makes it possible for [the viewer] to see a truth that he has never seen before' (1974, p. 10); Keats' 'negative capability' is cited in *Attention and Interpretation* (1970) as the basis for Bion's famous exhortation to the psychoanalyst: 'No memory, desire, understanding'; Milton's dark waters 'won from the void and formless infinite' illuminates distinctions between 'knowing' and 'becoming' O, Bion's signifier for ultimate reality (1965 p. 151); Leonardo's drawings of hair moving through water 'give a good idea of what [emotional] turbulence looks like' (1987, p. 224); Baudelaire, Shakespeare and Homer 'were able to penetrate states of mind which did not then exist – ours' (1987, p. 232). Meltzer ends his book *The Kleinian Development* (1978) with a personal note from Bion to himself, in which Bion, referring to Meltzer's phrase 'the aesthetic (beautiful) way' of organising clinical material, says:

Now I would use as a model: the diamond cutter's method of cutting a stone so that a ray of light entering the stone is reflected back by the same path in such a way that the light is augmented – the same 'free association' is reflected back by the same path, but with augmented 'brilliance'. (Meltzer, 1978, 3:126)

And in *Taming Wild Thoughts*, Bion reflects memorably upon the Sleeping Beauty as the hidden truth – the wisdom – that may elude the psychoanalytic practitioner who is led astray by the familiar and fascinating brambles of theory:

Think what a wonderful time we are all having, wandering about amongst the weeds, plucking the wild and beautiful flowers, admiring the brambles, the bushes, and not getting anywhere near to disturbing the sleep of the sleeping beauty – the wisdom that lies fast asleep somewhere in the thickets. (1997, p. 37).

As Meg Harris Williams says, in *The Aesthetic Development* (2010):

The only thing that changed in Bion's account of psychoanalytic evolution was his use of metaphor, which increasingly aligned itself to the world of art and fiction. Bion compares this evolution to the way that algebraic geometry lay 'implicit' in Euclidean geometry: 'that implicit truth was a kind of sleeping beauty waiting to be rescued ... the truth hadn't altered, it had become explicit.' (Williams, 2010, p. xxi)

Bion lamented the difficulties of language in conveying accurate meaning. He says:

Poets have found a method of communication ... Shakespeare strings together ordinary words in a way that starts things vibrating inside countless generations of people ... How is it done? (in Williams, 2010, p. 163)

He speaks of his wish to find a psychoanalytic language that, like that of a 'real poet' is both 'penetrating and durable'. 'I would like to be able to use language that did the same' (1980,

p. 64). For many of us, he came close to succeeding in this wish. This despite the fact that his prose style is far from easy, and is sometimes accused of downright impenetrability. As Meltzer says in his erudite, and frequently amusing, seminars to the Tavistock Institute:

> Reading Bion is perhaps not very different from being in one of his groups, where his fearlessness takes the form of a playful patience in the interest of allowing others to have experiences. The reader is so exposed to those experiences that he has not the slightest difficulty in believing in the impatience and exasperation of the members of the group when faced with this immovable body. (Meltzer, 1978, 3: 3).

This is a patience for which one may feel less than grateful. But the reader who can exercise his or her own patience, and become familiarised with Bion's style, is well rewarded. The importance for Bion of the aesthetic dimension is indeed powerfully conveyed in the manner of his writing.

It is Meg Harris Williams who has most fully set out the aesthetic parameters of Bion's thinking, and it is through her clear reflections, rather than Bion's own somewhat scattered ones, that I here present certain of his key ideas. His profound concern with the relations between science, art and religion, for instance, produces this metaphor:

> Galileo's telescope, with its poetic history (and its context of persecution by institutionalised religion) is often invoked by Bion as the sensuous counterpart of the faculty of 'intuition' to illustrate the type of mental instrument for which the thinker or psychoanalyst needs to find a suprasensuous analogy. We need to develop a 'psychoanalytically augmented intuition' to be the equivalent of the physician's 'see, touch, smell, hear' (1970, p. 7); in other words, an aesthetic dimension, in the sense that the term 'aesthetic' was coined originally, as that which then gives rise to the subjective experience of beauty. (Williams, 2010, p. 9).

She tells us he was 'profoundly impressed by the mental reorientation embodied' in Milton's lines on his blindness:

Shine inward, and the mind through all her powers
Irradiate, there plant eyes ... That I may see and tell
Of things invisible to mortal sight. (*Paradise Lost*, III: 51–54).

From these lines, describing how 'the inner light dawns and forcefully irradiates his mind', Bion took 'many of his own metaphors for alternative ways of knowing ... such as the sculpture whose solid structure acts as a "trap for light" ... or the rough and ugly surfaces in which an "idea might lodge", by contrast with the smooth continuum of scientific logicality' (Williams, p. 10).

The changes brought about by such insights are those that Bion called 'catastrophic': those shifts in the mind, frequently resisted, that alter our perceptions and thinking, whether on a great or small scale. This, says Williams, is 'by its very nature, an aesthetic experience ... the sense-based phenomena which carry through this type of knowledge are the "facts of feeling", which are intuitively discovered by the light of "attention", as in the analogy with Galileo's telescope' (p. 11).

Williams quotes Bion's close colleague, the psychoanalyst Martha Harris who was originally his supervisee (and who was also Harris Williams' mother):

Like Keats and many another poet [Bion] seems to regard truth as inevitably linked with beauty, and became in later years increasingly concerned with the problem of giving some fitting expression to the poetry of intimate personal relationships. (Harris, cited in Williams, 2010, p. 19)

Harris quoted Bion as saying that psychoanalytic interpretations would be much improved if they 'stood up to aesthetic criticism', meaning:

They would be *closer to the truth*. It is the feeling of beauty which is growth inducing, inspiring. This is what organises the different vertices, the conflicting emotions, into a meaningful pattern; this is what enables ... symbol formation to take place. The feeling of psychoanalytic conviction belongs to the domain of the aesthetic, or, as Keats said, 'I never feel certain of any truth but from a clear perception of its Beauty.' (Williams, 2010, p. 19)

This cluster of quotations may suffice to show the way in which Bion, often glancingly and allusively, illuminates the weighty intellectual arguments by which he expounds the 'theory of thinking' that aims to encompass the totality of the growth of human mental life. Contemplating this evidence, in addition to the grand claims he made for the importance of the aesthetic dimension, the reader may become puzzled that the aesthetic aspect of Bion's work has not been given greater recognition by other writers. It is as though this dimension were manifestly present throughout his thinking, and is in certain respects made explicit; but not in ways that can readily be presented in accounts of his theorising. As I have suggested, Bion himself has certainly played a part here, in a lack of any obvious sustained focus on the aesthetic realm. Most notably, it is absent altogether from the famous – or notorious – 'Grid', by which he attempted a quasi-mathematical formulation for the development of thought – an attempt he himself roundly denounced later in his life.

Perhaps Bion's speaking so little of beauty is no accident, but rather an expression of his respect for something that cannot be encompassed in words. But the omission of the aesthetic implications of his work from the literature is undoubtedly an example of beauty's absence, and does suggest something of a blind eye.

Aesthetic Conflict

As the first psychoanalyst to pay sustained attention to beauty and the beautiful, Donald Meltzer, as we have seen, gives it due celebration. But the story he tells is not one of unalloyed goodness. Besides the influences already recorded – his observation of his patients' differing attitudes to beauty, and his grasp of the implications of Bion's theories for aesthetic development – there was a further factor, and one that triggered some of his most original thinking. This was his own research with autistic children, a closely-observed study in which he and his colleagues established the influential theory of 'two-dimensionality', a phenomenon Meltzer has evocatively called 'the shallowing of the world of meaning'. In his book *Explorations in Autism* (1975) he draws out the significance of the intense aesthetic sensibility these children often displayed in their otherwise arrested state. His observations led him to believe that their limited and scattered 'two-dimensional' responses represented a profound withdrawal, whereby they had actually dismantled aspects of their sensory apparatus. Such 'dismantling' and 'shallowing' of response clearly suggest flight: a retreat, Meltzer believed, from the strength of an emotional response that was too much for them to bear. This response was to a beauty – that of the 'aesthetic object' – they had found overwhelming. It engendered in them a conflict between the outward appearance of that beauty and the uncertainty, and therefore mistrust, of its inner goodness. This conflict, Meltzer came to believe, is one universally experienced. Most babies survive it, indeed grow from it. The autistic children he studied, having suffered so extreme a response, possibly due to their very capacity for acute aesthetic awareness, had failed to do so.

In *The Apprehension of Beauty,* in seeking to establish his idea of the 'aesthetic object' as central to development, Meltzer, like Bion, traces 'proto-aesthetic' experiences to the womb: 'rocked in the cradle of the deep of his mother's graceful walk; lulled by the music of her voice set against the syncopation of his own heart-beat and hers; responding in dance like a little seal' (1988, p. 17). Nor does he ignore darker aspects: 'maternal anxiety may also transmit itself through heartbeat, rigidity, trembling, jarring movements … maternal fatigue may transmit itself by … graceless movement' (p. 17).

Such experiences, aesthetically pleasing or discordant, are succeeded by 'the bombardment of colour, form and patterned sound of such augmented intensity as greets the new-born'. For Meltzer, this will be overwhelmingly an experience of beauty and goodness. The phantasy quoted earlier, of emergence from the womb to a world of 'huge and beautiful creatures' powerfully evokes the scene. This is the primordial vision of the miracle of life as it appears to one coming from darkness to brightness and love, to holding arms, smiling eyes, and the wonder of the feeding breast: 'the period of maximal beatification between mother and baby'. Irresistibly invoked here is the experience of falling in love.

There is an obvious objection to Meltzer's claim, in that newborns are generally expected to cry lustily! For a fuller account see Meltzer's foreword to Harris Williams' *The Vale of Soulmaking* (2005), in which he imagines the 'panic and ecstasy' of being born (p. xvii).

So it is that Meltzer's 'ordinary beautiful baby, with his ordinary devoted beautiful mother' will – ordinarily – have an early experience resulting in the establishment of the 'aesthetic object': that unconscious imago of internalised beauty and goodness, nourished at the breast, and developing in the growing mind as it is fed by later experience. Meltzer cites fairy tales, cultural heroes and religious mythology as 'the traditional means, with their graphic, musical and dance modes of expression, by which the individual imagination is augmented' (1988, p. 151).

Meltzer insists on the intensity of the mother-baby encounter as the basis for the coming intensity of inevitable conflict:

> The picture of madonna-and-child is not always very enduring, but it is deeply convincing. One can see its power repeated in later years when a grandmother holds her distressed grandchild, waiting for its mother to return to feed it; thirty years drop from her visage as the bliss of success in calming the child spreads through her being. It is this moment when the ordinary beautiful devoted mother holds her ordinary beautiful baby and they are lost in the aesthetic impact of one another that I wish to establish in all its power – and all its after-image of pain. (1988, p. 26)

For, very early, another process takes hold – one driven, as it were, by the very nature of beauty itself. The baby cannot escape that other deep characteristic of beauty, its enigmatic quality:

> But the meaning of his mother's behaviour, of the appearance and disappearance of the breast and of the light in her eyes, of a face over which emotions pass like the shadows of clouds over the landscape, are unknown to him ... [She] is enig-

matic to him … he must wait for decisions from the 'castle' of his mother's inner world. He is naturally on guard against unbridled optimism and trust, for has he not already had one dubious experience at her hands, from which he either escaped or was expelled … Truly she giveth and she taketh away, both of good and bad things. He cannot tell whether she is Beatrice or his Belle Dame Sans Merci. (1988, p. 22)

Here is the reframing of the familiar paranoid-schizoid dilemmas in terms that are essentially aesthetic, and are based in the eternal doubt: can this beauty be trusted? In Meltzer's interpretation, this state arises as 'the consequence of [the baby's] closing down his perceptual apertures against the dazzle of the sunrise. In Plato's terms he would hasten back into the cave' (p. 28). Hence the double meaning of the deliberately-chosen word 'apprehension' in Meltzer's title. Rilke's line comes to mind: 'For beauty is nothing but the beginning of terror, which we still are just able to endure.' And we may perhaps paraphrase Eliot to suggest that humankind cannot bear very much beauty. The 'dismantling' of sensory and emotional response p erformed by the autistic child takes place to a greater or lesser degree within us all.

In creating his theory, the Kleinian Meltzer went so far as to suggest that, as a primarily sensory creature, the baby's earliest negative impulses need not be construed in terms of a death drive, or of innate envy, but as arising from painful or frightening sensory/emotional experience, giving rise to body-based negative emotionality. Thus he founds his aesthetic conflict in Bion's formulations, whereby the 'positive links' generated by the drives toward love (L) and knowledge (K) are pitted against the 'negative links' of minus L and minus K, that seek to deny and spoil truthful experience and expression. In the aesthetic conflict, the K link that longs to know the inside of the mother versus the minus K doubt of her inner goodness are the driving forces. Meltzer again reaches for the poet:

Toleration of this conflict … resides in the capacity that Bion, after Keats, has called 'negative capability': the ability to remain in uncertainty without 'irritably reaching after fact and reason' … In the struggle against the cynical power of the negative links this capacity to tolerate uncertainty, not knowing, the 'cloud of unknowing', is constantly called upon in the passion of intimate relations and is at the heart of the matter of aesthetic conflict. (p. 20)

A further implication of Meltzer's argument is that emphasis now shifts from conflicts engendered by the absent object to those arising from uncertainty about the present object. And yet more radically, Meltzer's newborn is the inheritor of a vision of the truth and beauty of the world before it is split into good and bad experiences – before, with the advent of the paranoid-schizoid position, now seen as being actually engendered by the aesthetic conflict, the original innocence is lost.[1] Once again we hear the echoes of mythical, poetic and religious versions of the pristine human condition.

One way and another, Meltzer's formulations concerning the dilemmas of early childhood do present certain challenges to Kleinian theory. The comment on the Melanie Klein Trust's website is appropriately cautious in referring to his

revised picture of early infancy, in which the 'aesthetic conflict', that is the impact on the baby of encountering the 'beauty and mystery' of mother, was placed at the beginning of life, and the Kleinian account of paranoid-schizoid phenomena seen as a defensive retreat from this. Perhaps the contemporary view would be that the subtle variations in the forms of mother-baby relationships are so numerous that these ideas are not alternatives but likely to be of differential centrality and to come to the fore at different times in the individual case.

Indeed, Meltzer's passionately-made claims sought not so much to overturn Klein's thinking as to augment it. He focused on beauty because of its sensory nature, but for him beauty and love, and the love of truth, are aspects of a total emotional response; and the essence of his case, following Bion, is one of emotionality versus anti-emotionality. To retreat from beauty is

---

1 Note parallels here with other theories, such as Ogden's sensory-based autistic-contiguous phase and Rycroft's state of 'primary integration'.

simultaneously to retreat from love and from truth. Such a retreat, the alternative to the path of growth through accepting and embracing the two-edged sword of beauty, is emotional stunting:

> The psychopathology which we study and allege to treat has its primary basis in the flight from the pain of the aesthetic conflict … [deriving from] the underlying, fundamental process of avoidance of the impact of the beauty of the world and of passionate intimacy with another human being. (1988, p. 29)

Meltzer's ideas have caught the imagination of many in the field, and carry what might be called the anthropological support of the near-ubiquitous myth of the garden of Eden. They capture recognised aspects of the human condition, in which the 'shades of the prison house' must inevitably darken the early 'clouds of glory'. The way through is that of aesthetic reciprocity, a concept that holds great significance for the psychoanalytic encounter and for Meltzer's (1967) 'beauty of the method'.

The rise of the aesthetic perspective:
Bion and beyond (2)

Recent contributions

B ion and Meltzer have been highly influential in open-
ing up debate on the aesthetic dimensions of mind. Of
the many who have contributed with insights of their
own, the leading place undoubtedly belongs to Meg Harris
Williams, to whom a separate section is given below. Others
are briefly reviewed here, though the selection is by no means
exhaustive, and I have confined myself to those I have found
most relevant. Of these, Meira Likierman deserves particular
mention as one of the first to be influenced by Bion's thinking.
In her paper quoted earlier she cites him in several contexts,
and amplifies some of his ideas along lines distinctively her
own, especially on the intimate relation of aesthetic to ethical
development.

More recently, the Argentinian psychoanalyst Lia Pistiner de
Cortinas' book *The Aesthetic Dimension of the Mind: Variations
on a Theme of Bion* (2009) is heralded by James Grotstein in his
Preface as 'almost encyclopaedically' reviewing all Bion's work
from the aesthetic vertex. She lays down strong foundations
for understanding the growth of mind through aesthetic

apprehension – her work will be further noted in the context of beauty and knowing.

Nicky Glover, in the aforementioned *Psychoanalytic Aesthetics* (2009), comprehensively surveys the field from the perspective of creativity and the arts. Her thinking is both scholarly and imaginative. Her wide selection of theorists and practitioners overlaps extensively with those named in this book, often with light shed on their beliefs concerning not only the creative capacity but the nature of aesthetic apprehension itself. Speaking, for instance, of the 'aesthetic encounter', she says of viewers of a work of art that they

> enter into the 'potential space' between the art object and the private world of fantasy (Winnicott) and engage in aesthetic reciprocity with the object – thinking 'with' rather than merely 'about' it (Meltzer and Williams) ... [They] imaginatively re-create aspects of the work encountered; they employ the same kind of creative perception as that which produced the work (Ehrenzweig). (Glover, 2009, p. xiv)

Sian Ellis's masterly essay 'Apprehending the translucent in the art of supervision', which won the 2017 Roszika Parker prize, deserves mention, not because it is overtly concerned with beauty but because it uses the (undoubtedly beautiful) work of an artist, Richard Diebenkorn, to illustrate a therapeutic process: that of the multiple and subtle dimensions in the 'art' of supervision. Ellis shows how Diebenkron's landscape series 'Ocean Park', in which the original strongly-stated ideas in the early paintings are gradually transformed, becoming increasingly opaque and translucent in the later works, can be seen as a metaphor for the supervisory process:

> In these translucent areas it is possible to imagine something of those original forms through lines and colours that seem to float up from underneath. The invisible becomes partially glimpsed and can be explored intuitively and creatively. (Ellis, 2017, p. 307)

The meanings Ellis draws are dense and hard to paraphrase, but in essence she is envisaging a supervisor able to create a safe frame, like that of the picture, within which to allow the 'translucent' space and freedom for the supervisory pair to 'think and dream and be alive to what is occurring' (citing Ogden). 'The final aesthetic will always contain the original', but the 'many stages of re-working' enable exploration of the 'alive and vivid landscape of analytic relationship' (p. 308).

In the States, George Hagman's book *Aesthetic Experience: Beauty, Creativity and the Search for the Ideal* (2005) reviews psychoanalytic contributions to the subject of 'aesthetic experience', defined by him as 'a phenomenon … that is felt to possess perfection or ideal form' (p. 15) – effectively then, beauty itself. Writing from the perspective of the 'developmental-relational' model, including self psychology, his emphasis on experience of the ideal within the mother-baby bond as the originator of the sense of beauty suggests strong affinity with Likierman's thinking. Yet the difference in underlying orientation produces corresponding differences (more or less subtle) in language and meaning from those of Likierman. And despite his assertion that it is the mother 'whose beauty is the first compelling aesthetic organisation', there is no acknowledgment here of Meltzer's work. For the British reader, many of Hagman's ideas, though they tally closely with familiar ones, and clearly refer to the same, or similar, phenomena, may yet give an overall impression more reminiscent of what we would think of as psychology rather than psychoanalysis. This however should not detract from the welcome breadth of his contribution.

A number of Meltzer's own supervisees and colleagues have written up their findings. Gianna Williams, in 'Reflections on "aesthetic reciprocity"' (2000), is concerned with aesthetic reciprocity and aesthetic conflict in her clinical work. Though cautious about Meltzer's claims for the universality of very early reciprocity, she confirms from her experience in baby observation sessions that 'an ecstatic and awe-inspiring feeling of aesthetic reciprocity between mother and baby can bowl over the observer in the earliest observations.' And she notes that she has become 'particularly sensitive to the first signs of recoiling from this overwhelming experience in mothers and babies, clinicians, and patients alike' (p. 143). Miriam Botbol Acreche's 'Daily beauty and daily ugliness' (2000) uses Shakespeare's designation of Cassio's 'daily beauty' to explore the analyst's work in the light of beauty and ugliness. Some of her reflections on 'ugliness' and 'beauty in practice' are included in the later sections of this book. In *The Newborn in the Intensive Care Unit* (1994), a study tracing the progress of premature infants, Romana Negri shows that their viability can be clearly related to their sensing that they are experienced as 'beautiful'. And Meltzer describes Giuliana Fortunato's session with her eight-year-old patient Claudia, who, deeply damaged by feeling herself perceived as an 'ugly little clown', actually drew a clown and then begged her therapist to throw it away, it was so ugly. Fortunato refused to do so, explaining that she believed the clown represented something valuable about Claudia that she wanted to understand. Movingly, Claudia was restored to her capacity for interest and understanding, so showing herself, as Meltzer says, 'a beautiful little patient for her therapist' on account of the beauty of her enquiring mind (Meltzer, 1988, p. 54).

Finally, a wide range of therapists document their clinical experiences in Meg Harris Williams' compilation *Aesthetic Conflict and its Clinical Relevance* (2018). Their descriptions of patients struggling with difficulties that can be interpreted under the broad umbrella of the aesthetic conflict brings home both the intense relevance of the aesthetic dimension to people's lives and the remarkable capacity of the concept of aesthetic conflict to explain the resultant problems. These case studies lend conviction to Williams' claim that this concept is one capable of being 'all you know and all you need to know' in terms of its potentially great explanatory power as a psychoanalytic paradigm – one ready now to take its place amongst the rich variety of others in our field.

Meg Harris Williams

Most prominent in this new literature are the many books and papers of the artist and scholar of literature Meg Harris Williams. Deeply grounded in the thinking of Meltzer and Bion – through family connection as well as her extensive psychoanalytic and aesthetic knowledge – Williams' work constitutes something of a tour de force, drawing from the fields of psychoanalysis, aesthetics, literature and myth to illuminate the new ideas that are beginning to inform our field. The concepts of beauty and the beautiful are intrinsic to her themes, not least in a written style expressive of her sensitivity and fluency as an artist. Informed by wide literary knowledge, she seeks to reveal the affinities between psychoanalysis and all aspects of aesthetic understanding and expression, including the arts themselves.

I single out her book *The Aesthetic Development: the Poetic Spirit of Psychoanalysis* (2010) as particularly relevant to my theme. This is an exploration of the work of Bion and Meltzer from the aesthetic viewpoint – and a call, based in their thinking and her own, for psychoanalysis to be understood primarily as an art form. This would not by any means preclude the rigour of what Bion calls the 'scientific vertex' – to the contrary, the art and the science of psychoanalytic theory and practice are essential to one another – but holds that the 'artistic vertex' is that more fundamental to our philosophy and practice. The arts, like religion, are our forebears: 'The emotional composition of the mind is traditionally the field of interest of artistic disciplines such as music and poetry, which employ sensuous means to convey mental abstraction' (p. 2).

Williams pursues the theme of the arts, as capable of direct expression of the truths that psychoanalysis seeks to discover, through examples from poetry and other art forms. She suggests the need in the analyst 'to keep listening for the psychoanalytic music or poetry, for its commanding form or underlying idea' (p. 163). And she quotes Bion's wish, noted earlier, to find a psychoanalytic language that, like that of a 'real poet' is 'penetrating and durable' (p. 161), and that, like Shakespeare's, 'starts things vibrating' (p. 163). Poetry, she says, 'with its centuries of experience in symbolising mind-to-mind queries and revelations of the type we call "self-analytic", can help direct attention to the poetic spirit that exists within psychoanalysis itself, and thus enhance its operation' (p. xxii).

Williams' argument ranges widely, but centres in three characteristics she believes intrinsic to the nature of both psychoanalysis and art. These are: the capacity for symbol formation, the phenomenon of inspiration, and the 'psycho-analytic dream encounter' between patient and analyst which she likens to the encounter between the artist and the work of art. Each is considered briefly here.

Symbol formation

In an extended reflection on the nature of symbolism and the innate human capacity for symbol creation, Williams comes to focus on the symbol in 'the complex artistic sense' articulated by the philosopher Susanne Langer. Here the idea held in the artist's imagination is conveyed through symbols that are capable of generating profound emotional meaning, and that carry the potential to point beyond themselves to still further meanings. Williams notes Milton's 'Idea of the beautiful', to be 'sought through all the shapes and forms of things' (p. 61) and says Langer suggests such a symbol 'articulates not just individual feelings but the "life of feeling" itself, the principle that underlies their individuation' (p. 57). She cites Langer: 'To understand the idea in a work of art is more like having a new experience than like entertaining a new proposition' (p. 58).

Such are the symbols derived during the process of psycho-analysis, whereby imagery and metaphor are gathered through the discourse of patient and analyst. Williams opens her book with just such a metaphor, quoting Bion's reflection on the Sleeping Beauty as the hidden truth that may elude the hapless analyst intent on pursuit of the 'brambles' of theory. In the chapter she devotes to the theme, Williams presents this meta-phor as an example of Meltzer's 'aesthetic object' – originally the internalised imago of the beauty of the breast/mother, and therefore of the infant's world, that constitutes our first experience of the beautiful. Here the aesthetic object is psycho-analysis itself, containing as it does the 'sleeping' meanings that Meltzer says are to be 'read' by both analyst and patient', or in Williams' words:

> Our improved understanding of the process as an 'aesthetic object' leads to a new conception of the psychoanalytic

method as an art form in which two minds together read this aesthetic object, and each gain in self-knowledge. (2010, p. 133)

Williams draws out the concept of the 'sleeping' aesthetic object through the richly symbolic poetry of Keats, who 'lov'd the principle of beauty in all things'. She lays out with a scholar's eye the complexities of meaning in the great 'art symbols' contained in the odes to the Nightingale and the Grecian Urn. As she does so, we can hear the parallels with our own discipline in her careful elucidation. Of the 'Nightingale', 'through listening to the underlying musical Idea, the poet makes contact with the unknown or unseeable inside of the object – the invisible spirit of the Sleeping Beauty through "viewless wing"':

> The sound of the song, which the poet is in a sense transcribing, impels him to investigate further. In the ensuing transpositions he pursues various means of union with the Nightingale, advancing and retracting, always learning something about the nature of his identifications and their incompleteness or false notes. (p. 94).

The encounter leaves the poet 'still with his aching heart but one that is fed with meaning'. The generative symbol of the Nightingale's song is 'the spirit of poetry' that will lead him out of despair into a new recognition of his own calling that will in its turn feed future 'hungry generations'.

By contrast, the 'Sleeping Beauty' of the Grecian Urn, which has 'slept for centuries and acquired an aura of the eternal in its sleep' is, Williams suggests, its very silence; while yet through its capacity to inspire a beautiful idea, it speaks of the lasting verities of truth and beauty that lie behind the flux of human struggle depicted on its surface. Keats' awareness of loss as he contemplates human transience is 'the foundation for a new orientation of the poet towards the object ... Now there is a new identification with the Urn, and a new sense of purpose for himself as poet' (p. 104).

Thus do the symbols of the Nightingale and the Urn, the one through the music of living song, the other through silent stone and dead civilisations, generate profound meaning from emotional experience. The matrix in which such symbols arise is that which poets call the Muse. The psychoanalytic equivalent, for Williams, is Bion's O, which he likens to the Platonic Form, the 'absolute essence'; and which he uses 'to represent this central feature of every situation that the psychoanalyst has to meet. With this he must be at one; with the evolution of this he must identify' (Bion, cited in Williams, p. 62).

Inspiration

Drawn from the Muse as is breath from the air, the poet's inspiration is recognised as a phenomenon that comes, or is felt to come, from a source beyond oneself. So it is for the analyst when insights arrive without conscious thought. We understand such insights to arise from unconscious processes taking place within and between ourselves and our patients; these seem often literally to be visited upon us, bringing to mind Bion's 'thoughts in search of a thinker'. A hallmark of such visitations is their perceived trustworthiness: they may surprise, but both poet and analyst recognise their truthfulness, and feel able safely to give expression to them in word or action. Described in another way, as it often is by the poets, such inspiration may be felt to call upon us to *obey* – though for the analyst this must where possible find assent also from conscious thought.

What then may be the source of 'inspiration'? Here I draw on Williams' book *The Vale of Soulmaking: the Post-Kleinian Model of the Mind* (2005). She makes clear that for her the Muse is not a metaphor only – it is 'a faithful description of the internal identification with a teaching object or deity' (p. 4). These good internal objects – Meltzer's 'household gods' –[1] are understood by Bion and Meltzer to be 'in a continuous process of qualitative evolution'. Through this process they 'intuitively absorb

1   Milner describes the term 'internal object' as 'that clumsy name for it': Meltzer's metaphorical 'lares et penates' may not be a viable alternative, but is certainly more graceful.

(introject) the qualities of admired figures in the context of circumstances that demand an expansion of their knowledge and capabilities' (p. 3).

Inspiration so construed, then, describes 'the process by which the mind is fed by its internal objects' (2010, p. 70). It is this process that generates Bion's 'learning from experience', in which he 'directs attention to the increase of knowledge in the sense of wisdom or understanding (Williams, 2005, p. 3). Similarly, the poet's emotional experience requires 'to become known to outer levels of consciousness in a symbolic form such that they can be thought about. This process of "becoming known" takes place under the aegis of the Muse, or internal object in psychoanalytic terms' (p. 4).

The process is an eminently natural one. 'Feeding, breathing, dreaming – these are the consistent, eternal metaphors used by the poets to set the scene for inspiration' (2010, p. 70). By the same token, however, inspiration does not materialise magically: the context is one in which the poet/artist/analyst 'has done his utmost to collect all the knowledge and experience he has had so far … His previous knowledge is the springboard from which he leaps' (p. 71).

And in order for the inspiration, the Muse, to come into play, it is necessary also to bring oneself into a state of careful attentiveness. This, and its concomitant, accurate observation, is a quality stressed by poets and analysts alike. Williams cites Keats' deep attention to the beauty of the Urn and the singing of the Nightingale, before he can be visited by the inspiration that carries him deeper into the meanings he is now able to imagine: 'beyond the beautiful surface to the underlying artistic principles' (2020, p. 103). He has entered 'the eternal process of learning from the object through inspiration and internalisation' (p. 106). This clearly parallels the analytic encounter, of which Bion particularly emphasised the importance of attention and observation.

Williams' language is that of Bion and Meltzer, but the 'teaching object or deity' clearly has much in common with Freud's concept, much developed by later thinkers, of the 'ego ideal'. Speaking of creative achievement, Janine Chasseguet-Smirgel in *The Ego Ideal* (1985) says:

There is no … artist, scholar, writer or thinker – who has not had some model, some mentor, some spiritual father. It is as if, in the realm of creativity, the most beautiful and most unusual flower is that which also has its roots deep in the soil of tradition. The great innovators have known the inspiration of being with those on to whom they have projected their ego ideal and whom they wish to resemble. (Chasseguet-Smirgel, 1985, p. 99)

Whether an inspiration comes from a source attributable to one of the concepts described above, or, still more mysteriously, from some 'thought in search of a thinker' must remain open to further understanding, or to our own musing minds.

The analytic dream encounter

This concept relies on Meltzer's definition of 'dream-life', whereby dreaming is by no means confined to sleep (in which dreams are 'the tip of the iceberg'), but continues throughout waking life in a form 'coextensive with Melanie Klein's "unconscious phantasy".' Dream-life, says Williams, 'continuously generates the meanings which we then apply to our view of the world. In this sense, dreams are not separate entities, but weave into one another as the story of our inner life' (2010, p. 140).

Seen in this light, the analyst's reverie may be said to take the form of a dream 'that contains the reflected meaning of the patient's emotional experience' (*ibid.*, p. 19). This is the 'counter-transference dream' by which the analyst may be enabled to hear the 'musical deep grammar' of what is being related – or 'dreamed' – by the patient, a state that Williams calls 'symbolic congruence' with the aesthetic object of the psychoanalytic process. 'How does the analyst know what he is talking about? [asks Meltzer]. He doesn't – he is "counter-dreaming"; he has, in fact, abandoned "thinking" (science) for intuition (art, poetry): the verbal tradition of Homer' (Meltzer, in Williams, 2005, p. 182).

This is Bion's 'psychoanalytically-based intuition' which we need to develop in place of the physician's 'see, touch, smell, hear'. Williams says:

Artistic intuition, reverie, counter-dreaming, is a sharpened attentiveness that overrides the tendency to omnipotently explain that can hamper the scientific vertex, or the tendency to moralise that hampers the religious vertex. (2010, p. 21)

For Williams, the scenario of dream life is to be understood in terms of the aesthetic conflict, whereby 'dreams are how we deal with our aesthetic experience; they embody our absorption of – or locate our turning away from – the beauty of the world and its manifestations' (p. 140).

Symbol formation, inspiration and the 'dream encounter' are, then, aesthetically-based ways of perceiving, experiencing and enacting that are held in common by psychoanalysis and the arts. Insofar as we are in tune with the 'music and poetry', the intuitively-known dream-life that underlies the session, so far do we share the insight of the artist who interprets the inmost apprehensions of feeling and finds ways to express these where they may be heard and seen by those ready to receive them.

Williams says:

Our aesthetic responses in all areas are founded on the origi-nal, primordial knowledge attained by the infant's first per-ception of the beauty of the world as seen in the mother or breast-as-combined-object. So, the goal of the psychoana-lytic encounter becomes that of restoring or reshaping any points of thwarted or stunted growth. (2010, p. xv)

'Restoring and reshaping' call to mind the artist at work; of the 'thwarted or stunted growth' that may stand in need of such work, Harris Williams quotes her father Roland Harris – no mean poet – with a couple of his lines:

Growth is the principle of our beauty,
Striving to speak the inward sense of things.

To this she adds: 'This quest to reconnect with the "inward sense" that makes our lives beautiful is achieved not through direct action on the part of the analyst but, rather, by facilitat-ing renewed contact with the mind-feeding roots of the psycho-analytic method as aesthetic object' (p. xvi).

CHAPTER SIX

David: Aesthetic Conflict[1]

D avid, in his early to mid fifties at the time of his therapy, had since early adolescence experienced occasional intense states triggered by the sudden apprehension of beauty in nature. In these, he felt himself enter a distinct change of being, one that had a trance-like quality to it. Over time, he had discovered descriptions that told him others experienced similar states, sometimes though not necessarily so closely associated with beauty or nature. These included, for instance, Berenson's 'aesthetic moment', the Shamanic 'non-ordinary reality', and, of particular interest to David, the phenomenon of 'nature mysticism'. A hallmark of such states – including those, like Aldous Huxley's, entered through drugs – is that while they last, they are experienced as self-evidently the 'real'. 'Ordinary' reality is felt to be one-dimensional and mundane, a state to which one is reluctant to return. A further key characteristic is a deep sense of *knowledge* of the object of the experience.

---

1 A version of this chapter was first published in *Aesthetic Conflict and its Clinical Applications,* ed. M. H. Williams (2018). as 'I see, not feel, how beautiful they are'.

Here is an extract from something David wrote when trying to describe such an experience:

> I am sitting on the side of a gorge. My eyes light on a fragment of the cliff opposite, half-lit by morning sun. The fragment is a chiaroscuro of light and shade, shapes and curves in the rock, and colours – greys, russets and deep greens shading to darkness. I move into the state of being held in the beauty. No words attach to this state, but by deliberately scanning another part of my mind, I can find the words 'delight' and 'knowledge'. These though add no meaning to the experience itself – they are not relevant to it, and I return with relief to the state of simple seeing. Not that 'simple' is the word either. It is almost infinitely complex, multi-layered; holding intense significance both in its minutest detail and as a whole. I cannot articulate the significance, but if I imagine the fragment removed and placed in a frame in an art gallery, its beauty and meaning immediately fall away. So it cannot be form, line and colour alone I am experiencing. There is a gestalt that holds the fragment in a multitude of perceptions that I can only describe as 'knowledge'.

David explained that when he used the words 'I move into the state of being held', this was to be taken as having a precise meaning. Something actually took place, though the 'movement' was not self-initiated: it happened to him, and could not be experienced at will. It was as though he found himself suddenly locked into something, entranced. The state might last only a few moments – or rarely, if he were fortunate, for much longer.

It is unusual, in my experience, for patients to bring the subject of beauty as a major theme in their therapy. In searching for material that might illustrate aesthetic conflict, one might expect to look elliptically, perhaps for themes in which beauty may be implicit, or for evidence shown through what Donald Meltzer called 'the beauty of the method'. David, though, pursued the theme as a thread that ran through his material for a fairly sustained period. Unsurprisingly, the conflicts he experienced around beauty were symptomatic of, and mirrored in, other significant aspects of his pathology. Where beauty itself

was concerned, evidence of conflict appeared in certain prob-
lematic encounters with things and places he found beautiful.
Such encounters were not far to seek. While the particularly
intense episodes described above were comparatively infre-
quent, David was generally sensitive to beauty in many forms,
and had a frequent and frustrating experience of being with
others in a beautiful place, or looking at beautiful things, and
finding his response out of tune with that of the others. He
would attempt to experience the beauty in a way he felt to be
commensurate with its demands on him, and was then aston-
ished that others seemed not to be taking the time to make the
same attempt. Not uncommonly, he found himself in trouble
with a group of others because of dawdling, taking 'too long'
over things and holding people up. He learned to spend his
time alone when he was seeking beauty, which was increasingly
often as he grew older.

A deeper, and related, problem was the condition of feeling
'cut off' from the beauty he sought. He used to quote from
Coleridge's 'Dejection: an Ode', in which the poet, having
described an evening scene of great beauty, yet finds himself
seeing it 'with how blank an eye':

> And those thin clouds above, in flakes and bars,
> That give away their motion to the stars; ...
> Yon crescent Moon, as fixed as if it grew
> In its own cloudless, starless lake of blue;
> I see them all so excellently fair,
> I see, not feel, how beautiful they are! (ll. 31–37)

Being thus able to perceive beauty so accurately, yet find oneself
unable to *feel* it, was an experience painfully familiar to David.
He held moreover a particular fear that others were able to move
so lightly past beautiful things because they were apprehending
them easily and naturally, where he so often had to wait, and
even struggle to 'feel'. Where he failed to do so, this was made
harder to bear by self-condemnation for his own inadequacy. The
conviction that he lacked something others possessed alternated
with the possibility of its opposite – that he in fact loved and
experienced beauty, and therefore felt its absence, to an unusual

degree. Either way, he was too often unable to realise this aspect of himself, and to make the connection he longed for.

This inability to connect with what he desired was symptomatic of other experiences of alienation, and for the most part his therapy was concerned with these. Meanwhile, the focus on actual beauty provided much that can be interpreted in terms of Meltzer's thinking, and in particular his concept of 'aesthetic conflict'.

The answering activity

David knew the work of Marion Milner, and in her book *Eternity's Sunrise* (1987) he found ideas that seemed to him directly to address the search on which he was engaged. Milner's 'answering activity' held strong resonances of what he could sometimes feel in response to beauty. Though she does not explicitly tie this intensely personal phenomenon to the experience of beauty as such, beauty is frequently present or implied; her encounter with the beauty of the Parthenon, described earlier, is particularly evocative of what she means by this 'answering' that arose in her so powerfully in response to something outside herself. She describes how over the years she learned, through her 'wide attention' and through ways of 'deliberately turning contemplative attention inward into one's body', to encourage the response of the 'answering activity'.

Such transitional experience of close interrelationship between self and other, enhanced by illusion, grows, according to Milner, from the mother-baby 'fused' state of which she was so aware, and which so interested her in the matter of aesthetic creativity. This fusion, or its derivative, Berenson seems clearly to describe as the 'aesthetic moment'. For him though this was a state not accessible at will. Nor, it seemed, was such a possibility open to David, who must wait until the experience was granted, despite his attempts to follow Milner's practices. For that matter, it was not always possible for Milner either: often there were times when there was no 'answer' from her inner world. She speculated: was it 'the remains of infantile splitting that could be preventing one finding the good Mother Nature in one's own body more consistently?' (p. 46). Or was it the unconscious belief that one 'had killed the source of goodness, like the Ancient Mariner who killed the albatross ("and answer came there none")?' Or perhaps, recalling her visit to the virgin and child mosaic at Torcello, their mutual halo a symbol of their unity, 'denied grief, denial of the need to mourn, denial of the need to accept the loss of all that glory' (p. 58). She describes the couple:

> Here was the infant in glory, sharing the glory of the great Queen of Heaven ... Here surely then was the glory of before the taste of bitter grapes ... before realising one's utter dependency on one's mother. (Milner, 1987, p. 36)

This signals a conflict couched in aesthetic terms, and though Milner's wording refers to the depressive state of loss, rather than to conflict over the present object, there seem nevertheless clear echoes of the aesthetic conflict here.

Disrupted reciprocity

Following Milner, David visited the mosaic at Torcello and stood before it for a long time. It told him of a blessed early condition he was unsure of having experienced himself. Once, in a session with a body therapist, he had experienced a frightening, sharp-nosed face pushed closely into his own; in another, he fought desperately to get something or someone out of his chest. These incidents he grew to associate with a conviction of having been 'invaded' by a mother who undoubtedly adored him, but who seems also to have been adoring aspects of her own idealised self, projected into him with the intention of winning the love of his father through him.

Meltzer, speaking of 'the factors which encourage or inhibit the tendency of parents to see the newborn as an aesthetic object', believes this to be a 'delicately balanced situation', in which 'behind, in the background, and perhaps most important of all, is the quality of the parents' relation to one another, the degree of passion of their sexual union, the extent to which a child was yearned for' (1988, p. 56). No question that the child David was yearned for; the other factors though, as David knew, were sadly troubled, or lacking.

There are many psychological languages for experiences of invasion. Meltzer has given us one based in the idea of violation of private inner space, with corresponding degradation of intimate relationships. Here:

> Alertness to the manifestations of aesthetic conflict soon makes one recognise that the most important aspects of the degradation occur in this very dimension: degraded beauty of the objects and degraded capacity to experience the aesthetic impact in the self. (1988, p. 74).

For David, it seems evident there was a disruption of aesthetic reciprocity in the face of apparent, and indeed demanded, mutual aesthetic appreciation. And it is possible there was a further complicating factor here. David claimed that his mother was unusually beautiful, and a photograph gave clear evidence of this.

It may seem strange to suggest that a problem could arise from confrontation with an aesthetic object that is in fact recognisably 'beautiful'. We should expect all mothers to be beautiful, for the reasons Meltzer gives: 'her breast, her face, her embracing arms', and 'essentially her mother-liness, the manifestation of her interior qualities'. But developmental psychology, as we have seen, has something more to say here. In view of the research findings quoted earlier, it seems not impossible that the infant David felt an extra demand on him to appreciate his mother's (actual, 'formal') beauty, perhaps placing a further strain on reciprocity. Meltzer believes the reason that most babies manage to cope without pathological withdrawal from 'the dazzle of the sunrise' is by virtue of their belief, conveyed to them by their parents, in their own beauty. David provided possible evidence here, in his conviction that his mother possessed a beauty he had not inherited, and of which he felt a degree of envy.

The blow of beauty

Increasingly, David accepted the link between his very early experiences of beauty and the beauty he encountered in landscape. The maternal connotations of ('mother') nature are widely acknowledged. Of the landscapes David found beautiful, one he especially loved was that of limestone. He quoted Auden's 'In praise of limestone', in which the poet suggests it forms 'the one landscape that we, the inconstant ones,/ Are consistently homesick for'. He invites us to

> Mark these rounded slopes
> With their surface fragrance of thyme and beneath
> A secret system of caves and conduits
>   … examine this region
> Of short distances and definite places:
> What could be more like mother … (ll. 3–9)

David came to understand that he was able when in the more intense states to access an original experience of great beauty. Inasmuch as his 'trance' state held a strong element of recapture – of something Meltzer insists all babies must once have known, a first 'blow of beauty' – he recognised that, despite subsequent vicissitudes, he must once have known beauty in good measure. Hence the intensity of his love for it, and his distress at being separated from it. (Interestingly, the darker reaches of Auden's poem, in which 'this land in not the sweet home that it looks', is open to interpretation as variations on the aesthetic conflict.)

The experience of separation from beauty, as became gradually clear, signalled a powerful recoil. David well knew that his experience of being cut off from 'feeling' beauty held an ambivalent element: that his search was not altogether a wholehearted one. There was somewhere within him a doubt whereby he felt dimly that to be closely in touch with beauty was not something he entirely wanted. He grew to discern that a part of him was actually afraid of the feeling engendered by beauty: that it would be 'too much' for him, though of what he hardly knew. It was not until he found himself 'in' the beauty – 'on the other side of the line', as he put it – that he would find that fear ungrounded. Time and again, it would come as a surprise to him to discover that to be there was simple, natural, something that felt entirely good. Here surely were the effects of the aesthetic conflict at their most evident. The conclusion could only be that a part of himself had long ago retreated from the 'dazzle' and 'hastened back into the cave'; in adulthood, the cave-dweller clung still to the shadows on the wall in preference to the light outside, yet to be convinced of the safety and reliability of beauty's goodness.

Seeing and knowing

A time came when, with much of the foregoing discovered and supplying a framework to build on, a change took place in David's attitude to his therapy. Where before he had been tightly wrapped within his own narrative, to the extent that any contribution from outside himself was seen as potentially an interruption, he became more ready for interchange. This seemed to coincide with a growing sense of what he perceived to be beauty in his therapist.

Kenneth Wright's call, noted earlier, to 'put the human face back into psychoanalytic theory' (1991, p. 2) is echoed by Frances House in her paper 'The face of the therapist in psychotherapy practice' (2001). House describes the results of a small piece of research she conducted, inspired by a baby observation in which 'his mother's face seemed to be the most beautiful thing in his universe', and a 'love conversation' took place in which, 'transfixed by delight', he never took his eyes away from her face. House draws together evidence to show the potential importance to the patient of the therapist's face, both as reflecting that of the original mother and as presenting the possibility of an alternative experience. She notes Winnicott's (1971) suggestion that the whole of therapy, 'a long term giving back to the patient what the patient brings', is in fact 'a complex derivative of the face that reflects what is there to be seen.'

To be seen – and to be known. Wright's words are worth quoting again in the context of the important link between aesthetic apprehension and cognitive development with his words: 'I like to think … that the mother's face gets into the baby's experience, not only as the cherished centre of his world, but simultaneously as the guiding light of his mind' (1991, p. 12).

The relation between seeing and knowing will be further explored in a later chapter. Suffice for now to say that the 'knowing' inherent in deep experiences of beauty was already familiar to David. Through what Milner calls a 'different kind of knowing' he had been to some degree 'initiated' into Berenson's 'illuminating, formative mysteries'. And mindful of the mysteries he had 'known', it was important to David that his experience of beauty be not reduced by being referred exclusively to the events of his infancy. While he could give clear assent to the idea of recapture, with its connotations of unconscious childhood phantasy, he was unsure of having felt the full emotional truth of it. For him, his relationship with the beauty he loved remained primarily that of the adult experience that pointed him toward spiritual growth. The task ahead, he felt, was of a reconciliation of adult with child self in the matter of a safe emergence from the 'cave'.

Aesthetic reciprocity

Being now in touch with a reliable source of beauty-as-goodness in his therapist, David was able to enter more fully into what Meltzer calls 'the beauty of the method'. Such a move is described by Gianna Williams in the (2000) account of her work with Matthew, an adolescent boy who felt 'not equipped to expose himself to the dazzle of the sunshine' of 'passionate intimacy with another human being'. A session came in which Matthew's 'appreciation of feeling understood … the "cloud of glory of his enquiring mind", his wish to be helped to give a meaning to his pain', created in his therapist a countertransference feeling that she expresses in Meltzer's words:

> For in the interplay of joy and pain engendering the Love (L) and Hate (H) links of ambivalence, it is the quest for

understanding, the K link, that rescues the relationship from impasse (G. P. Williams, 2000, p. 142).

Matthew in this session did not recoil from the beauty of the analytic experience. 'There was between us a truthful feeling of aesthetic reciprocity', says Williams. It was a feeling increasingly experienced in David's therapy.

Meltzer claims that important dreams come when the beauty of the method begins to be realised, and David brought a dream that seemed to him to mark a change:

He was in a foreign country, in a magnificent coastal scene that he surveyed with a sense of his own rightness in it, he being alone, on holiday and free to make the choices he wished. He had a sense of knowing what he was doing, and expecting to do it well. He looked along the coast, and seemed to pick out some promising omens, including the distinctive paving slabs of a restaurant he was familiar with and liked. He set out to walk down the coast with the feeling that he had strayed serendipitously into a remarkable scene. When he reached the slabs, however, he couldn't find the restaurant – it seemed he had been mistaken.

The scene changed, and he was looking through some travel magazines. He saw a number of places he badly wanted to go to, that very year: he felt the intense pull of them, but knew such travel was out of the question. Then he thought, daringly, why not? It came to him then, still in the dream, that he had changed – yes, he wanted to travel, but somehow now for different reasons than before, though he was unsure exactly what they were.

Then he was again in the great coastal scene, now going toward a beach. He became aware that a mother and child were alongside him, bound for the rocks that lay a little way out to sea, wanting to swim from them as he had watched them doing before. The mother was saying what a wonderful place this was, and seemed to be inviting him to go with them. Looking out to sea, he saw there were now enormous swells rising from it, like small mountains, and pointed them out – the mother agreed, the rocks had become something very different. The waves reared vastly, and broke – stupendous, terrifying. Again came wonder at the marvellousness of this land.

David was struck both by the vividness of the dream and by the familiarity of some of its themes: the love of travel; of being alone and being good at it; of awe at the beauty of landscape. But more striking still was the evidence of difference and change. The familiar restaurant was not there; his motives for travel had changed in some way; and he was ready to dare adventures he had thought beyond him. The woman and child he had originally watched from a distance became his companions, so that instead of marvelling alone he found himself exclaiming together with them at the magnificence and strangeness of the scene. And that scene itself underwent a dramatic change. Gone were the accessible rocks, safe for swimming from; their place was taken by wild and tempestuous waves that displayed a threatening aspect to their beauty. The familiar landscape that had hitherto fed him (the restaurant) had become one less safe but still more amazing: it now suggested danger on a grand scale, but also a marvellous one.

The vision of (mother) nature wearing both her dangerous and beautiful aspects simultaneously came after the omnipotent single traveller had joined with others – significantly enough a mother and child. There is clear evidence here of the workings of Bion's 'new idea' embodied in 'catastrophic' change. This idea is, necessarily, feared. Harris Williams points out that where Meltzer claims the new idea presents itself as 'an "emotional experience" of the beauty of the world and its wondrous organisation', the implication must be that it is feared 'for *the impact of its beauty*' (2005, p. 192). David, though deeply thrilled by the waves, did not feel fear of them. Here surely is the aesthetic conflict made endurable, indeed embraceable, through communion with the mother in aesthetic reciprocity.

CHAPTER SEVEN

Beauty and Knowing (1)

David would have well understood Schiller's lovely line: 'Only through Beauty's morning gate, dost thou enter the land of Knowledge' (*Die Künstler*). His more intense experiences of beauty were bound up with what he described as a deep sense of knowing that which he perceived. Such 'knowing' may be described as insight, or a kind of deep understanding. Knowledge of this sort is clearly related to the idea of wisdom, which has been closely associated with beauty since the time of Socrates and beyond. Plato, already quoted as saying that a man should live in contemplation of absolute beauty, for 'in that region alone will he be in contact not with a reflection but with the truth', seemed unsure whether to name Beauty or Wisdom as the greatest of the Forms. He gives the impression that any apparent distinction between them was as irrelevant for him as that between beauty and truth for Keats, who simply equated the two.

This deep connection between beauty and truth, and its significance for our profession, has been a continuing thread throughout this book, and is implicit in much of the thinking of the more recent psychoanalysts included here. Since however the two concepts are extremely broad in their scope, a closer examination of their meanings seems now called for.

Schiller, and Keats after him, were speaking of experience at an exceptionally deep level, one that belongs to our spiritual life – Bion's 'religious vertex'. This is what David used to call 'the second kind of knowing', and Milner spoke of as 'a different kind of knowing'. Such knowledge is itself doubtless beyond analysis. It might be thought of as a sense of completely apprehending that which one is seeing (or otherwise sensing), though this is a description unlikely to satisfy the experiencer. Subject and object seem in some way to join, suggesting Milner's 'fusion'. David did not fully accept the latter word, since it sounded to him too much like complete merger, which did not feel accurate. While he readily accepted that the state was trance-like, he insisted that such fusion as took place was only partial: he retained a clear sense of his conscious self throughout. Perhaps a third element, or agency, is felt to be implied. Berenson's 'initiation' into 'illuminating, exalting, formative mysteries' suggests as much; and David when in such states found himself often visited by Wordsworth's phrase 'a sense sublime of something far more deeply interfused'. Overall though, the experience defies ordinary description. We must leave it to the poets to speak here.

The close affinity between beauty and knowing is not however confined to such profound experience. Beauty is perceived at many levels, including that of simple recognition: 'That's beautiful!', the knowing of Meltzer's 'donné'. At any level, beauty is inseparable from knowing, not least because we inevitably 'know' beauty itself. James Kirwan says that beauty is 'the one thing we do "know" absolutely, its being is to be perceived, and thus it guarantees its own reality'; for 'the perception of beauty is so immediate as to leave no room for enquiry … in the realm of beauty, *esse* is *percipi*' (1999, p. 5). He quotes Hume as saying that since the perception of beauty is 'determined by sentiment', it follows that my 'judgement' of beauty is infallible (p. 5). And he says of Kant's doctrine that when taken to its essence, it proves to be: 'if it feels like beauty, it is beauty'.

There are many channels, sensory and otherwise, by which beauty is perceived, but it is no accident that the emphasis in this chapter (and indeed the whole book, as noted in my Introduction) is primarily on the sense of sight. The immediacy of the connection between eye and mind is most familiarly expressed by the simple words 'I see'. 'Our soul is made for thinking, that is, for perceiving', said Montesquieu. Physiologically speaking, the eyes are part of the brain to a greater extent than any other of our senses, not least in terms of the actual quantity of cortex devoted to the visual. Here is the physical basis for Freud's concept of *schaulust*. Leon Wurmser elaborates on the connection Freud made: 'On an archaic level the equation exists: seeing = knowing = thinking'; 'curiosity, the sublimated interest in knowledge, in research, in investigation, as well as in beauty, leads back to scopophilic wishes' (Wurmser, 1981, p. 149).

Thus it was Freud, as usual, who set the psychoanalytic stage for this set of concepts, though as noted, his 'scopophilic drive' is now associated more often with pathology than with the powerful human longing for knowledge. It was left to Klein to recognise the infant as epistemophile, and to Bion to give to Knowledge a place alongside Love and Hate as having primacy amongst the drives. These insights have led to a recognition of the interdependence of the epistemophilic drive and visual apprehension on a scale far greater than Freud could have envisaged. As Nicky Glover observes, 'Bion stressed that it was the visual sense that lies at the core of unconscious phantasy, and he describes the phenomenology of the analytic encounter more and more in terms of visual and aesthetic analogies' (2009, p. 127). Citing just such an analogy, James Grotstein in *A Beam of Intense Darkness* uses Bion's example of an artist painting a path through a field of poppies, to illustrate his concept of transformations. The painter reconfigures the original poppy field into something very different indeed – namely, pigment on a piece of canvas – yet still 'something has remained unaltered and on this something recognition depends'. Grotstein comments that Bion himself painted landscapes and so was well able to understand the comparison. He adds: 'Perhaps we can go a step further with the analogy to say that the mind generally, and the unconscious specifically, is a portrait and landscape painter'. This mind, as artist, is able to transform 'raw Truth' by 'consulting his inner aesthetic capacities and knowledge of the laws and hidden order of aesthetics' (a reference to Ehrenzweig's *Hidden Order of Art*):

> Our hidden painter paints by day and by night to get the proper angles and perspectives and the ratios and mixtures between fiction and truth of life's existential assembly line. Consequently, everything we see, hear, smell, touch, think, and feel constitutes an 'artistic painting'. (Grotstein, 2007, p. 218)

To return to the time of Freud, and to the broader connection between aesthetics and knowledge, it is interesting to note that a parallel understanding was growing in the field of aesthetics itself. Writing at the turn of the 20th century, the highly influential Italian philosopher of aesthetics Benedetto Croce produced a theory that convincingly founds the twin concepts of aesthetic perception and knowledge in early experience. His account in *Aesthetic* seems strikingly sympathetic to psychoanalytic thinking. Originally, he says, incoming sensations create 'impressions' on the mind: these impressions he defines as 'emotionality not aesthetically elaborated' (1909, p. 15). The necessary elaboration takes place through the mental activity of the imagination – or in Croce's language, 'fantasia'. The result is what Croce calls 'aesthetic knowledge', or, interchangeably, 'intuitive knowledge'. Based as it is in the human capacity to generate imagery, this knowledge need not be of the 'real': 'Intuition is the undifferentiated unity of the perception of the real and of the simple image of the possible' (p. 4). All this, says Croce, is prior to logical, or conceptual, knowledge, and is its necessary ground, for without imagery we cannot create concepts. Thus he establishes the aesthetic/intuitive mode as the ground of our knowledge, its primary mode. Such knowledge, though interwoven with conceptual knowledge, is not dependent upon it, but has its own autonomy.

The parallels with Kleinian and post-Kleinian understanding seem evident, not least in the foreshadowing of unconscious phantasy and the part it plays in mental growth. It suggests too the Bionic description of the development of thought in order to comprehend sensory and emotional states. 'My intuition tells me what I experience, suffer or desire', says Croce, and for him the apprehension of a poem or other work of art consists essentially in 'contemplation of feeling'.

Meira Likierman, building her case for aesthetic knowledge as primary rather than proceeding from the depressive, echoes Croce where she says that 'the pre-conceptual world' is experienced aesthetically, so that 'thereafter the aesthetic aspect of the object remains that which is known other than through the thinking mind' (1989, p. 138}.She gives the example of a soft attractive light that is in one sense merely a phenomenon pleasurable to the senses but which, crucially, 'the mind captures and represents internally'. She adds that 'aesthetic knowledge is decisive to our ability as a species to represent the world to ourselves, that is, form a phantasy life with which to imagine and think' (p. 134).

Psychoanalysis has deeply plumbed and elaborated the world of Croce's 'imagination'. In particular, Pistiner de Cortinas' aforementioned work (2009) explores the implications of Bion's 'aesthetic vertex'. In the course of an investigation into the severe damage to symbol formation in her autistic and psychotic patients, a damage that obstructs the development of 'phantasies, dreams and dream thoughts', she considers in great detail the origins of symbolisation, and produces convincing reasons why we should see the aesthetic capacity as primary and foundational for the early life of the mind. She describes the way in which alpha function transforms both sensory impressions and emotional experiences into visual imagery appropriate for mental storage, whence it can be presented to consciousness, and the experience it represents be 'discovered, thought and given a meaning'. In this way each of us creates a personal 'alphabet' of images formed through sensory and emotional conjunctions; these combine in different forms, able to evoke past, present and future experiences, and forming the 'eyes of the mind' that are needed for imagination and insight.

These 'eyes' are needed also for aesthetic judgement in the Kantian sense, whereby we are able to discern that which we find beautiful. Since, as Kirwan points out, such 'judgements' are in fact instantaneous – donné – they are perhaps better described as recognitions, with judgement simply implied in the outcome: 'That's beautiful!'.

To look more closely at the capacity for such discernment – such 'knowing' that a thing is beautiful – I return to a point I noted in my introduction: that of beauty's appearing to us to inhere in the object, though we can know it only subjectively. It seems thus to lie rather mysteriously athwart the inner and outer worlds. Here possibly the baby experiments quoted earlier may have light to shed. The researchers were convinced that the babies were responding with a preference, apparently inborn, for certain aesthetic qualities in the faces shown. Here apparently not only inner subjectivity but in some way also an external object was playing a part. It is in fact, as the researchers decided, difficult to explain the findings in any other way.

Could this offer a possible template for later experience? Clearly it would not do to extrapolate too freely from this very early scenario, which may be a 'special case'. Any particular aptitudes shown by babies will hardly surprise the psychoanalyst who has long recognised the mental propensities and awarenesses with which the human infant is born, and will expect these to apply particularly to key elements in the holding environment, not least the mother's face. But we may perhaps speculate that it is the very nature of that early interchange, containing the first and therefore the deepest impressions on the mind and brain, that may create – or perpetuate – aesthetic templates that continue into later life.

If we allow the possibility suggested by the researchers that, in the visual field at least, an object or quality might indeed have some 'independent' aesthetic appeal, we must look beyond 'the eye of the beholder' as the sole instigator of the experience of beauty. But what might such 'independence' mean? Not, presumably, that an object can meaningfully possess beauty in the absence of an eye, or potential eye, to behold it. Rather, we would be looking at an innate predisposition of the human mind to find certain things beautiful: that is, some kind of *correlation* between mind and object. This formulation clearly has the potential to marry the 'inner' and 'outer' aspects of the experience of beauty.

Needless to say, this will not be a new idea: as has been said in countless ways, no idea is ever new. Winnicott said, disarmingly enough in view of the sheer originality of his output: 'naturally, if what I say has truth in it, it will already have been dealt with by the world's poets (1974, p. 103). Only the context of an idea may have changed sufficiently to open up new possibilities for thinking about it. In the case of the correlation I am suggesting, the question of the aesthetic relationship between subject and object is a familiar one in the philosophy of aesthetics, and Kant himself had much to say about it. His theories are endlessly disputed, and allow for multiple interpretations, but I note the comments of Emily Brady, a leading figure in the field of environmental aesthetics, in her delightful book *Aesthetics of the Natural Environment*. Using Kant's own example of the contemplation of a flower, she says:

> Finding the flower beautiful is a direct consequence of an *accordance* or *attunement* between the perceptual qualities of the flower and the mental powers which Kant calls the imagination and the understanding ... Kant thus characterises beauty as the appreciation of something through an immediate encounter between an appreciator and a particular object. For this reason, we have no predetermined concept of beauty; it is something that arises in a *relationship* between subject and object. [my italics] (Brady, 2003, p. 33)

Brady herself recognises aesthetic qualities in the object as 'real' – and therefore defensible in aesthetic judgement – while holding that their existence is 'importantly dependent on the relation between the appreciator and the object'.

Though these philosophical points cannot be said to address my argument directly, they do suggest some pointers for the subject/object relationship that use words sympathetic to the idea of a 'correlation'. They offer an area of speculation that is, again, beyond the scope of this book. Of more relevance perhaps is Segal's idea that a key component of beauty is a 'rhythmical' quality, quoting Herbert Read as saying that such rhythms correspond to 'the way we are built and our bodies work'. Inasmuch as these rhythms are certainly universal, Segal's point seems to reinforce, albeit on a narrow basis, the idea of an inbuilt concordance between mind and object, arising from biological processes we all necessarily experience.

While as yet we lack the necessary knowledge, neurological and otherwise, to substantiate the idea of 'correlation', it may hold enough apparent validity for us to consider some aspects of its likely nature.

One obvious result would be considerable agreement as to what is beautiful. This perhaps is more widespread than current debates about historic and cultural difference would suggest. In my experience, those objects, both natural and created, held by a given culture to be most beautiful are found beautiful also across other cultures. This seems true of fields other than the visual – as in music, in nature, or in the world of ideas. Examples come to mind rapidly and almost randomly, and the images multiply: the moon and stars reflected in a lake, a Rembrandt portrait, a Native American sculpture, Japanese painting, Indian music, the great dance of Lascaux, quince blossom, a spray of fractals. It may be that Kant's point that to perceive beauty is to expect others to do the same – the claim to 'universal validity' – will be found to be not simply a wish, but based in a degree of reality!

Kant, of course, used the word 'taste' when speaking of judgements of beauty. The word has come to have a rather different meaning today, and one likely to produce far greater divergence in what people find attractive. This however is not necessarily relevant to the subject of beauty as I am considering it here. Taste as we now understand the word suggests a kind of appreciation that could be influenced by a great many 'interested' factors, as opposed to the pure 'disinterest' of the experience of beauty.

A further characteristic of such a correlation is likely to be that sense of recognition so often felt by experiencers of beauty. Where an object or quality excites a pre-existing disposition to find it beautiful, there must be a sense of already 'knowing' the beauty that is perceived. This, paradoxically, in no way rules out the element of surprise that seems also to be an inevitable characteristic of beauty: it comes upon one unlooked for, yet unmistakeable.

I end these speculations with some words from Bion. Speaking of Plato's Forms, he notes that phenomena such as the appearance of a beautiful object 'serve to "remind" the beholder of the beauty of the good which was, but is no longer, known' – that is, it is recollected. Hence, he says, 'I claim Plato as a supporter for the pre-conception, the Kleinian internal object, the inborn anticipation' (1965, p. 138). Not quite the language of the laboratory researchers, but not so far either from the meaning behind their claims: that some recognition of beauty is inborn.

So is beauty known to us, and so, to a greater or lesser extent, does it enable us to access knowledge, or truth, beyond itself.

A note on ugliness

Some day, I doubt not, we shall arrive at an understanding of the evolution of the aesthetic faculty; but all the understanding in the world will neither increase nor diminish the force of the intuition that this is beautiful and that is ugly. (T. H. Huxley, 1894)

Given that we 'know' beauty through direct recognition, it follows that we shall 'know' beauty's opposite, ugliness. And as with perceptions of beauty, we may expect that disagreeable or discordant sensations and experiences will create a perception of ugliness, or its equivalent, from very early in life. Rather than accepting Segal's contention that experience of ugliness arises chiefly from the conflicting emotions of the depressive positon, we should now expect that position rather to enable some reconciliation between the pre-existing poles of beauty and ugliness. This would in fact be compatible with Segal's claim that beauty must contain within itself the element of ugliness in order to be whole – or 'real' – that is, not simply pretty.

This is an understanding long recognised. In the article quoted earlier, Donald Kuspit notes that St. Augustine held beauty to be a compound of opposites, including ugliness and disorder; and that 'God is an artist who employs antitheses of good and evil to form the beauty of the universe' (2002, p. 11). Kuspit goes on to consider Francis Bacon's declaration that 'There is no excellent beauty that hath not some strangeness in the proportion' ('Of Beauty', 1625). Kuspit finds this 'strangeness' – which he also calls 'uncanny', recalling Freud's speculations on the subject – has its meaning revealed by psychoanalytic understanding. Things seem strange or ugly to the conscious mind because they derive from unconscious desires and fears. As Williams says, 'The hidden inner beauty of ideas seems ugly and monstrous to the existing mind that does not want to become changed' (2010, p. 35).

Bion too says that 'built-in ugliness' is a necessary feature of transformations in beauty. As he frequently pointed out, a chief component of this 'ugliness' derives from fear. Milton, Wordsworth and Rilke have all referred to beauty as containing terror. And Williams notes the play between the 'sublime' and the 'beautiful' in 18th century aesthetics: 'pleasant beauty is counterpointed to the Longinian sublime type of beauty with its associations with fear and defamiliarisation ... undermining our preconceptions of what is harmonious' (2010, p, 35). Of the analytic process itself, she says:

> The idea of "beauty" here is thus a complex one that contains within it the sense of ugliness and monstrosity. As Shakespeare put it in relation to Caliban: "this thing of darkness I acknowledge mine" (*The Tempest*, V.i.275). The therapeutic capacity of the aesthetic (beautiful) object does not result from denaturing the ugliness of destructive or painful emotions (as is sometimes said); on the contrary, the object retains its dangerous qualities. (2010, p. 34)

(recalling the dangerous waves in David's dream).

The interplay between beauty and ugliness displays another of its characteristics in Rodin's phrase, quoted by both Segal and Kuspit, concerning a 'magic wand' that 'transfigures' ugliness into beauty. A classic example occurs in Coleridge's *Ancient Mariner,* when the water snakes, the erstwhile 'thousand thousand slimy things', become in the moonlight suddenly beautiful to the Mariner's eyes. At the sight of that beauty,

> A spring of love gushed from my heart,
> And I blessed them unaware.

This recalls Von Balthasar's claim for beauty as holding a leading place amongst the transcendentals: it is the beauty that penetrates the Mariner's despair, followed 'unaware' by the 'spring of love'. Not so much a 'magic wand', then, as the natural awakening by beauty of renewed emotionality. Harris Williams sets ugliness in the context of Meltzer's aesthetic conflict, retreat from which leads to the anti-emotionality of minus L, H and K – a realm that the Mariner had until then so wretchedly inhabited.

Meltzer and Harris Williams (1988) claim that at the heart of anti-emotionality lie 'cynicism, perversity and vulgarisation of taste'. Harris Williams quotes Iago's bitter perception that Cassio has 'a daily beauty in his life / That makes me ugly'. This beauty, says Harris Williams, is, in fact, sincerity. 'Cynicism is ugly in itself, since it exists only to block off the possibility of truthful knowledge' (2005, p. 153). Very much in the same vein, Rodin wrote in a tirade against the 'false and artificial': 'When an artist, intending to improve upon nature, adds green to the springtime, rose to the sunrise, carmine to young lips, he creates ugliness because he lies' (1911).

Miriam Botbol Acreche takes up this theme in her aforementioned paper 'Daily beauty and daily ugliness' (2000), its title inspired by Iago's outburst. For her, the ugliest part of Iago is not his hate and envy (feelings at least 'human') but his cold-bloodedness. 'The horrible aspect in Iago, his "ugliness" is his lack of feelings ... the coldness of his machinations'. She reflects on the impact of ugliness in our work:

> Although analysts in their consulting rooms are not artists or thinkers as Bion or Meltzer are, they can fight from their own daily trenches to avoid being swallowed by the 'ugly' monsters of hopelessness or vain illusion, or becoming hardened with a routine 'armour-plating' (Bion) before beauty. (Botbol, 2000, p. 7)

Fortunately for little Claudia, the child so memorably described by Meltzer as perceiving herself through her mother's eyes as an 'ugly little clown', her therapist was not so 'armour-plated'. Though Claudia was indeed far from physically attractive, her therapist's perception of the beauty of a mind that longed to understand enabled her to be recognised as 'a beautiful little patient'. 'The ugliness that has been in the eye of the beholder is lifted when the doors of perception are cleansed', says Harris Williams, using Blake's phrase (2005, p. 32). It would be nice to think that Claudia might have read the children's classic *The Velveteen Rabbit*, with its message that 'once you are Real you can't be ugly'.

CHAPTER EIGHT

Beauty and Knowing (2)

Beauty in practice

In creating his phrase 'the beauty of the method', Meltzer gave a poetic name to something recognisable by most who practise our profession. He says in the introduction to *The Apprehension of Beauty* that the book is

> intended as a celebration of the beauty of the method which Freud discovered and developed, a method that enables two people to have the most interesting conversation in the world, hour by hour, for years, and to relinquish it with regret owing to the imperative of psychic reality. In doing this, in celebrating the beauty of the method, we are, in fact, celebrating the beauty of the method by which the mind – as a phenomenon made possible by the giant computer of the brain – operates upon the emotional experiences of our lives to give them a representation through symbol formation that makes thinking about these experiences possible. (Meltzer & Williams, 1988, p. xii)

And elsewhere he says:

> Not only had I become aware that the psychoanalytical method had taken on an aesthetic quality in my eyes but I had begun

to see, mainly through dreams, that it had done so for some of my patients as well. (Meltzer,[1986] 2018, p. 245)

Analysts, he suggests, should bear in mind that they are 'presiding over a process of great beauty'.

Meg Harris Williams has elaborated the concept. 'The method will be beautiful', she says, 'according as it is able to tap into the underlying dream life that is the truth of the emotional experience' (2010, p. 14). This will be when 'the aesthetic perspective finally becomes predominant, fusing and clarifying what had previously been tentative, implicit, obscured' (p. 191). 'The feeling of psychoanalytic conviction belongs to the domain of the aesthetic', says Harris Williams, and she quotes Keats as saying 'I never feel certain of any truth but from a clear perception of its beauty'.

While the whole psychoanalytic idea, and way of working, together with the principles that govern them, may be called beautiful, the phrase seems to belong particularly to a time that may happen when the method comes into its own and becomes, as it were, immanent in the process evolving between the two participants. This is the realisation of Meltzer's 'aesthetic reciprocity'. Here words or silences come seemingly from beyond conscious control; they belong to the moment, are harmonious, fitting, even inevitable. And there is a trust, or knowledge, that the other is equally in tune and will speak words that belong, to be responded to accordingly. The utterances are to be trusted because the source from which they arise is trustworthy. It is as though one were speaking in obedience to something independent of oneself, yet entirely oneself. This, one supposes, is, or closely approximates to, Bion's 'becoming' psychoanalysis.

Fit

Such attempts to describe the process are by their nature unsatisfactory. But a simple word that comes to mind is 'fit', or 'good', in the ancient Greek sense of right for purpose. This was the very same word the Greeks used for 'beautiful'. Leon Wurmser, in a section headed 'The feeling of fit', speaks of 'the feeling tone of insight' between analyst and patient, comparing such moments with the 'happiness described by artists when they have found the right form and by scientists when they have discovered the right formulation. In both instances a type of beauty is attained' (1981, p. 286). In all this is implied also that other characteristic of beauty, a sense of recognition – an experience that recalls Plato's 'recollection' of that which we have known before. Wurmser notes that 'Freud talked about the amazed feeling – "I have known that all along"' (p. 286). What is being recollected? Kenneth Wright relates the feeling of 'fit' directly to the 'fit' or otherwise of early mothering. He uses an example that brings to mind Bion's wish for 'poetic' diction:

> Why will one person fumble about in a clumsy way with words, grasping at the first word that comes to mind, irrespective of the fit or accuracy, while another person will use language creatively, with a freshness and accuracy of fit that convey vividly the needed meaning? (Wright,1991, p. 139).

'I think we could guess', says Wright, 'that the creative word is in direct descent from the symbiotic mother who closely adapted to her child's needs' (p. 139). This explanation we may find more sympathetic than the notion of recollecting a Platonic Form; though the two ideas are not necessarily incompatible, and may perhaps be seen to relate to each other in the light of Bion's 'ultimate reality'. Such a speculation however, in common with many others touched on here, is well beyond the scope of this book to explore.

The Aeolian Harp

Concepts like 'aesthetic reciprocity', 'tapping into the underlying dream life' and 'the feeling of fit' call for an image that will be more expressive than words. Here I choose that of the Aeolian harp, pictured on the cover of this book. Like any metaphor, its power to convey all it is designed to signify has limits, yet it can I think convey a good deal of the beauty of the method, more particularly of those moments in which the interchange between analyst and patient becomes harmonious, effortless and free. As a poetic metaphor, it is without doubt one of Langer's highly generative 'art symbols', and has indeed proved inspirational for artists of every kind. The image of the harp is one in which art and nature combine, to create what Coleridge calls 'a soft floating witchery of sound'. And D. H. Lawrence sang: 'Not I, not I, but the wind that blows through me!'

The analogy for our own work is of an openness to, and resonance with, the free-floating currents below the surface of the session (Bion's 'music and poetry') that may provide a key for something more profound than what is being talked about. Jung (1931) said:

> The utterances of the heart—unlike those of the discriminating intellect—always   relate to the whole. The heartstrings sing like an Aeolian harp only under the gentle breath of a mood, an intuition, which does not drown the song but listens. What the heart hears are the great, all-embracing things of life, the experiences which we do not arrange ourselves but which happen to us (Jung, *CW*, 15: 1719).

The harp has caught the imagination of those who have evolved a form of psychodynamic therapy they call the Aeolian Mode. Murray Cox and Alice Theilgaard, in their book *Mutative Metaphors in Psychotherapy: the Aeolian Mode* describe a way of listening for the metaphor in the patient's communications that confronts the therapist with an 'aesthetic imperative' – an 'irresistible summons' to respond, as the harp 'picks up the music of the wind'. This imperative they compare with a poet's claim that 'what needed to be said could not be expressed in any other way' (1987, p. 27). The therapist's 'associative resonance', and the patient's response, give them both 'augmented access to the patient's inner world [which] is catalysed by poetic association and poetic induction' (p. 55). Using this mode in their work with psychiatrically ill patients, Cox and Theilgaard say: 'an image could safely hold experience which was too painful, too brittle or too broken to be firm enough to tolerate psychoanalysis' (p. xiii). The mode is designed to bring about poesis, the process of 'calling something into existence that was not there before'. The writers cite Heidegger's examples, not only of the poet producing a poem, but also of 'the blooming of a blossom, the coming-out of a butterfly from a cocoon, the plummeting of a waterfall when the snow begins to melt'. Such things 'resonate with that within the patient which is called into existence' (p. 23).

Because of the fragile nature of their patients' mental states, the Aeolian Mode is more interventionist and 'supportive' than the psychoanalytic way of working. But its practitioners are working according to the same principles, and the metaphor of the harp is potentially applicable to many, perhaps all, forms of therapy, adapted according to the modality. Any therapist would recognise the language used by the writers: '[The Mode] facilitates response to the numerous nuances, and the hints of 'other things' which so often people the therapeutic space' (p. xxvi); '[The therapist's] response may take the form of a conventional intervention, but it may be a changed orchestration of an existing silence' (p. 28). And they quote Bachelard: 'The image has touched the depths before it stirs the surface' (p.xiii).

Interest

By comparison with all the above, 'interest' may seem a simple, even a mundane, idea. It is not, of course. Meltzer's description of the dialogue between patient and analyst as 'the most interesting conversation in the world' recalls John Turner's reflection on Winnicott's prose: a 'poetry of illusion' that 'generates interest'. Miriam Botbol Acreche says:

> When we encounter something that engages our interest, when we see it as a fragment for instance or sample of the beauty of the world, we wish to ascertain its authenticity, to know it in depth (Botbol, 2000, p. 7).

She claims it is this interest 'that helps us to bear the 'ugly' parts of our work', of which she cites 'feelings of disappointment, anxiety, incertitude'. Interest tides us through such feelings, since what we find interesting, naturally, has meaning for us. The deep engagement it generates seems to me an important ingredient of the beauty of the method. Alfred North Whitehead's delightful words come to mind: 'In the real world it is more important that a proposition be interesting than that it be true. The importance of truth is that it adds to the interest' (1929, p. 259).

I give the last words of this section to a fragment I found online (but have sadly been unable to retrace). It comes from a lecturer addressing his students on the subject of Freud's view of beauty as a sublimation of sexual feeling. This, he points out, contrasts with Plato's idea of beauty as Form, wherein the beautiful is the object, not the derivation, of eros. And interestingly he suggests that while the Greeks did not have a conception of the unconscious per se, for Plato the knowledge of beauty as a Form is largely submerged in subconscious knowledge, a truth that must be recollected. The lecturer concludes:

> But if we were to borrow from the Greek tradition, rather than from its modern development, Freud might be tempted to suggest that beauty is not so much a distraction from the truth of psychoanalytic theory, but the light that shines in the very confrontation of the conscious with the unconscious, and the intoxicating emergence of a truth (not a substitute feeling) that we find there.

The pantheistic vein

A theme that calls for inclusion here, though not directly addressed to psychoanalysis, is the love of beauty in nature that runs so deeply in human beings. Its relevance for us, apart from its being a near-universal characteristic of our natures, is in the way it brings together the twin concepts of beauty and knowledge.

I shall illustrate the theme through a number of quotations, hoping to bring out some of the ideas and passions that run through experiences of the beauty of the world of which we are part. The chosen passages reflect my own responses where their beauty of expression or meaning has caught my imagination. I leave them to speak for themselves, rather than attempt comment from the perspective of our profession,

I use the term 'pantheistic vein' to cover a very broad spectrum. The love of the natural world takes many forms, and I intend not only pantheism itself, the spiritual movement that understands the beauty of nature, from a flower to the stars, to be an expression of the divine (indeed, to *be* the divine, with no separate god envisaged); but also the various branches of nature mysticism, in which the beauty is likely to be seen as expressive of God, or gods; and finally that sheer love of natural beauty, with or without reference to the divine, which is itself expressive of spiritual aspects of our nature. It seems probable that all at base are charged with the same emotions of love of, and wonder at, the natural world. The fact that expressions of the divine are so widespread, with no necessary belief in God or gods, seems to reflect the intensity of feeling engendered, and especially the sense of awe.

This 'vein' can be traced back to humankind's earliest roots, to the prehistoric cave paintings which (as noted later) express both beauty and the spiritual. In historical times, a very early celebration of 'non-human beauty' in nature is exquisitely expressed by Euripides through the Maenads as they sing in the Orphic tradition, itself traceable back to the 6th century BC, its roots doubtless long before that. The poetry reflects the intimate relationship with the natural world intrinsic to the rites of these seekers after divine knowledge:

Will they ever come to me, ever again,
The long, long dances,
On through the dark till the dim stars wane?
Shall I feel the dew on my throat, and the stream
Of wind in my hair? Shall our white feet gleam
In the dim expanses?
O feet of the fawn to the greenwood fled,
Alone in the grass and the loveliness...
To the dear lone lands untroubled of men,
Where no voice sounds, and amid the shadowy green
The little things of the woodland live unseen.

(Euripides, *The Bacchae*, internet classics archive)

The love of beauty in nature may manifest in unexpected places. Earlier I quoted Freud's rather surprising eulogy of the countryside; another not renowned for his love of natural beauty, which is virtually absent from his philosophy, is Plato, who suddenly produces a similar outburst that seems almost uncannily to echo Freud's, two and a half millenia earlier, in its natural and unfeigned delight. Socrates is speaking of the grove in which he holds his dialogue with Phaedrus, 'a fair resting place full of summer sounds and scents':

> Here is this lofty and spreading plane tree and the Agnus
> Castus high and clustering, in the fullest blossom and the
> greatest fragrance; and the stream which flows beneath the
> plane tree is deliciously cold to the feet... How delightful
> is the breeze – so very sweet, and there is a sound in the air
> shrill and summer-like which makes answer to the chorus of
> the cicadas. But the greatest charm of all is the grass, like a
> pillow gently sloping to the head (Plato, 2005, p. 37).

Socrates speaks of a gentle and pleasing beauty, his tone correspondingly placid. Contrast another rural scene, equally gentle
in its nature, but experienced with vastly more passion. This is
in part because of the emotional state of the experiencer, but
is also carried by the perception that its beauty is initiated by,
and directed toward, God. George Orwell, that 'pious atheist'
(Gordon Bowker) imagines his way into the mind of a clergyman's daughter, who is escaping her miseries for a moment as
she does something as ordinary as kneeling in a summer field:

> Her heart welled with sudden joy. It was that mystical joy in
> the beauty of the earth and the very nature of things that she
> recognised, perhaps mistakenly, as the love of God. As she
> knelt there in the heat, the sweet odour and the drowsy hum
> of insects, it seemed to her that she could momentarily hear
> the mighty anthem of praise that the earth and all created
> things send up everlastingly to their maker. All vegetation,
> leaves, flowers, grass, shining, vibrating, crying out in their
> joy. Larks also chanting, choirs of larks invisible, dripping
> music from the sky. All the riches of summer, the warmth of
> the earth, the song of birds, the fume of cows, the droning
> of countless bees, mingling and ascending like the smoke of
> ever-burning altars. Therefore with Angels and Archangels!
> (Orwell, 1935, p. 53)

This reads so convincingly that Orwell seems to be speaking from himself. One suspects him of sheltering behind the
fictional persona he has created to express a 'something beyond'
to which he cannot himself give intellectual credence. It comes
perhaps from Milner's 'different kind of knowing'.

This different kind is certainly present in the writings of W. H.
Murray, who movingly captures the mountaineer's recognition

of the convergence of beauty and knowing. He describes a scene of extraordinary beauty on waking after a night spent on the peaks of the Cuillins. Of this he says:

> Beyond such bare words one may say little. The mind fails one how miserably and painfully before great beauty. It cannot understand. Yet it would contain more. Mercifully, it is by this very process of not understanding that one is allowed to understand much: for each one has within him 'the divine reason that sits at the helm of the soul', of which the head knows nothing. Find beauty; be still; and that faculty grows more surely than grain sown in season ... here, for the first time, broke upon me the unmistakeable intimation of a last reality underlying mountain beauty; and here, for the first time, it awakened within me a faculty of comprehension that had never before been exercised. (Murray, 1947, p. 4)

Later that day, the scenes he had witnessed

> suddenly fused in image of the beauty we had seen during the supreme hour [on the mountain]: so that I knew, what until then I had not known, that the one Beauty pervades all things according to their nature, they having beauty by virtue of participation in it; and in the degree of realising its presence within us, so is life lived in fullness. (p. 6)

Murray writes as a mountaineer, but what he has to say is strongly reminiscent of the accounts of acknowledged nature mystics. One such is Richard Jefferies, who, speaking of the great wealth of nature surrounding us and its capacity to influence the mind, which has 'immense power in it unused', says:

> Stoop and touch the earth, and receive its influence; touch the flower, and feel its life; face the wind, and have its meaning; let the sunlight fall on the open hand as if you could hold it. Something may be grasped from them all, invisible but strong. It is the sense of a wider existence – wider and higher. (Jefferies, 1909, p. 273)

These things create 'an increased consciousness of our own life. The stream of light – the rush of sweet wind – excites a deeper knowledge of the soul … let us receive more of the inner soul life which seeks and sighs for purest beauty' (p. 278).

The pursuit of knowledge in science has its own relationship with beauty. Henri Poincaré states the matter with simple certainty:

> The scientist does not study nature because it is useful to do so. He studies it because he takes pleasure in it, and he takes pleasure in it because it is beautiful. If nature were not beautiful, it would not be worth knowing, and life would not be worth living. (Poincaré, 1952, p. 48)

And we find Einstein giving voice to the increasing numbers of scientists who find themselves engulfed in mystery as the world of science opens before them new fields of unimaginable greatness. At times, he says, he feels himself freed from 'identification with human limitations and inadequacies. At such moments, one imagines that one stands on some spot of a small planet, gazing in amazement at the cold yet profoundly moving beauty of the eternal, the unfathomable' (in Bernstein, J., 1973, p. 11).

It is the unfathomable that Eric Dietrich addresses in his book *Excellent Beauty* (2015). Those things that cannot be fathomed, the great mysteries of existence, are for him intrinsically beautiful. He speaks of 'the beauty of seeing more than we can understand'. The term 'excellent beauty' he borrows from Francis Bacon, citing the latter's claim that such beauty invariably has 'some strangeness in the proportion', this to bring out the deep relationship he perceives between beauty and enduring mystery. Examples of such mysteries are 'the intractable existence of consciousness' and 'the strange behaviour of infinity' (p. 149). Not only have these not been understood by science but, he believes, they cannot by their nature ever be understood. He describes their manifestations at considerable length, backing his argument with explanations from his position as a philosopher with knowledge of an impressive range of subjects, from cognitive science through artificial intelligence to metaphysics. He finds such mysteries 'beautiful, profound, and unnerving, pointing to deeper truths that we have yet to embrace' (p. 147); 'once seen, they and their stark beauty are almost overwhelming ... they add an aesthetic dimension to our lives' – and he proposes 'an enduring mystery aesthetic' (p. 149). The universe, then, is 'richer, deeper, more magnificent' even than it appears. Dietrich believes it is the excellent beauties that will satisfy our longing for the divine in a post-theist age: 'Those willing to acknowledge the mysteries are genuine mysteries and to see their beauty are probably willing to go a little further and allow themselves to feel reverence toward the mysteries' (p. 151).

Such reverence takes us to a concept that may be said to pervade many of the foregoing extracts, from ancient to modern, from the love of the very small to that of the immense. This is the concept of the sublime, a complex idea with varying historical meanings, not all including beauty but generally used nowadays to describe a natural scene (or work of art, or idea) that inspires the sense not only of great beauty but of something more. There is an admixture of intense awe, even dread: this is the place where the terror sometimes associated with beauty comes into its own. Ronald Hepburn notes in his essay 'Landscape and the metaphysical imagination' that Alpine travellers were among the first to struggle to describe this

> memorable, powerful and perplexing range of experiences, which were of undoubted aesthetic value, yet were not experiences of beauty as understood in neoclassical aesthetic theory. They combined, or fused, dread at the overwhelming energies of nature and the vastnesses of space and time with a solemn delight or exhilaration. (Hepburn, 2004, p. 136)

And for Kant, the observer who sees

> massive mountains climbing skyward, deep gorges with raging streams in them, wastelands lying in deep shadow and inviting melancholy meditation ... is indeed seized by amazement bordering on terror, by horror and a sacred thrill. (Kant, 1987, p.129)

It is clear that great experiences of beauty and the sublime in the natural world call upon humankind to construe, to make some meaning of, the 'something more than we can understand', whether we do this in terms of the transcendent divine, the immanent divine, the reverence-inspiring excellent beauties, or some other signifier of the unknowable. All express our own spiritual nature confronted by a world of which we also are an (amazing) part.

To add a single comment from psychoanalysis, it is Bion who has come closest to expressing that which we can somehow apprehend but not understand, through his signifier 'O':

> It stands for the absolute truth in and of any object: it is assumed that this cannot be known by any human being; it can be known about, its presence can be recognized and felt, but it cannot be known. It is possible to be at one with it (1970, p. 30).

CHAPTER NINE

Mary: The Beauty of the Method

Miranda, you are to be wondered at:
through all your tempests, dark eyes round with fear,
you drifted on an uncharted ocean
where waves slapped emptily into dark caves
and no ships passed. Your raw screams, Miranda,
echoed eerily in my own heart's straits.
Sighting you, I knew my loss, wondering
that you were still alive. I said your name.
So at last, let me hold your face gently
to my cheek. Wrapped warm now in this soft shawl,
red-fringed, you have arrived perilously
home. Here sparkling foam crashes on a beach
glassed over with the wide sky's reflection,
and a fresh stream tumbles into the sea.

Miranda was a floppy doll, bought by Mary early in her therapy as we encountered memories of the intense fear and pain she had suffered as an eight month-old when left for three weeks in the care of an unloving grandmother. *The Tempest* provided her with apt metaphors for her inner state. The name Miranda, meaning 'worthy of admiration', seemed right at the time, but turned out to be a poor fit, since before long Miranda fell out of favour, largely because of her appearance. She was shop-bought, had an artificial face, was not truly like enough to her owner/mother/younger self. Mary knitted a replacement doll for herself, this time giving her the name of Amy, the beloved. Amy had the 'right' face: she was beautiful, while Miranda was unattractive, unappealing.

Amy became a constant companion, cherished and used in many ways; Miranda was relegated to the charity shop.

The work continued along a path that was indeed tempestuous. Pain, fear and grief figured largely, and it was not until some resolutions were being reached that I wondered aloud about the fate of Miranda. By this time, Mary was able to recognise her as a rejected, 'ugly' part of herself, and reacted with the compassion that inspired the poem above.

Important themes are touched on in the poem. The baby's terror and sense of emptiness; the rescue from great danger that therapy represented; the sense of homecoming after a long and perilous journey. Water appears in many moods: this was a theme that ran through the therapy in a series of symbols and metaphors that included seas, rivers, fountains, and often a beach or shore where land met sea: a potent symbol of the gradual reconciliations that were taking place.

Mary's sense of beauty was evoked for me time and again by the poems she brought: the vivid beauty of a scene; the auditory beauty of music; the beauty of the right, the fitting, word. Her rich use of symbol and metaphor was natural to her: she possessed in high degree Meltzer's 'poetic function' that 'finds the metaphoric means of describing the inner world through the forms of the eternal world' ([1976] 1994, p. 377). But most of all it was working with Mary that most clearly brought home to me the 'beauty of the method' of psychoanalysis. Many factors were at play here, but the overwhelming one was Mary's own relentless pursuit of emotional truth.

This pursuit was not obviously apparent at the beginning of therapy. She explained early on that she expected not to need therapy for long, that she was familiar with the concept of transference and was unlikely to give me much of a problem in that respect, as she was not inclined to project her difficulties onto others. It was not until eighteen months into the work that she suffered a sudden collapse in a Christmas break, and was from that point unable to repudiate her dependence on me. This grew into an intense need, so that all separations, including short ones, became hard for her to bear. Combined with increasing recognitions of the refinements of cruelty inflicted on her, unconsciously and otherwise, by her parents, she found herself prey to huge negative emotions that it took all her courage to face.

And a harsh story she certainly had to tell. Her memories of a childhood and youth spent at the hands of her depressed father and emotionally infantile mother gave her very evident pain to tell, and made difficult listening. In a family that maintained a pretence (half believed in) of loving closeness, many conflictual undercurrents were in play. A fragment from a poem 'To my parents' (both had died) is eloquent of their dependence on her, and the burden of their emotional demands:

> I wonder, do you know now in a new
> dimension how you mangled my being
> under the wheels of your out-of-control
> expectations skidding on the surface
> of love?

There was much more that echoed the dark metaphors in 'Miranda'. In a poem to her mother about the terrible experience of being left – effectively, abandoned – as a baby:

> Your face was wonderful at first; your jet
> black hair a fence around infinity.
> And so your loss was an infinite pit.
> You gave me the gift of language; even
> now words fail me in describing the hell
> of isolation.

The poem ends with her response to her mother's own 'poisoned words':

> I exiled my Self – a peace offering.

The trauma of abandonment and loss was greatly compounded by the death of her baby brother when Mary was only three years old. She perceived her parents as being completely unable to cope with the death, simply leaving him alone to die in his room. It suggested to her the dreadful possibility that they might be unable or unwilling to uphold her own life if it were threatened.

The 'exiled self' was eventually 'discovered' by Mary in the course of therapy. Her poem 'My baby is found' is a graphic telling of that experience. She captures the senselessness that the baby had somehow to make 'sense' of – by turning on herself, bad and ugly because abandoned:

> One dark night of terror,
> blinded by my fears,
> helplessly groping in obscurity,
> I find my baby,
> stumbling upon her in the abyss of hell.
>
> . . .
>
> This dark night of terror
> is my baby's badness;
> she is abandoned in hell
> because she's babyish;
> it is night because she doesn't matter.

And:

> *The refugee child*
>
> Was it only yesterday that I met
> a child, her brown eyes blank with wintry grief?
> She clutched her doll, whose woolly face bore the
> marks of astonishment at the child's pain.
>
> She was abused and exiled from her home;
> no whitewashing her character – she's bad
> and ugly…

That badness was of course intensified by the dread phantasy that she herself was in some way responsible for her brother's death.

Her later childhood experiences tended only to reinforce the underlying fears. Her mother's 'poisoned words' were those used in relentless attacks on her as an 'utterly selfish' child. In a written address to her, Mary described 'your deliberate, sadistic cruelty in systematically dismantling my sense of self', and quoted her: 'You're selfish to the core. It's self, self, self, first, last, and every one in between. You think of no-one but your own selfish self' – this to a seven year-old. Mary added: 'You were my self-appointed victim as well as my persecutor'. Her mother's 'thinly disguised envy' caused her to find intolerable her daughter's attempts to create a life for herself. This took such forms as shrill demands that Mary come and do the washing-up if discovered playing with her friends or absorbed in a book. Later, predictably, boyfriends were sneered at and discouraged.

As for her father, the deep self-absorption surrounding his depression, accompanied by intermittent threats of suicide, left him unable to give his daughter the fathering she needed. This did not prevent his expressing a heavy dependence upon her with such utterances as: 'I'll get better for *you*', as he put his arm around her, sobbing. She was 'horrified and repelled' by the contradictory implications of this. Speaking from the child's perspective, she writes: 'I am overwhelmed by the costliness of the gift promised to me.' Later his dependence took a new turn. Having long derided his daughter for stupidity, he discovered when she took the 11+ that she was in fact very bright. 'It is at this point that my daddy's depression becomes directly linked in inverse proportion to my academic achievement. I am no longer free to fail … any failure of mine "makes" him depressed.' The conflicting messages of derision and pressure to succeed continued, becoming 'almost paralysing' while Mary was taking her degree at university.

A remarkable feature of the work was Mary's ability to enter earlier versions of her self with an immediate knowledge of them, rather than simply remembering them, so that she was able to inhabit them, as it were, directly, and to allow them to speak for themselves, as in the example above. She wrote many prose pieces in the first person. One describes the baby's experience of being fed by her grandmother when her parents, in an act described by Mary as 'desperately wrong', left her for three weeks while they moved house to another town. It is a detailed and moving account of an eight-month-old's acute distress and despair, apparently unsuspected by the adults. I give here a few brief extracts, starting with the disastrous first feed in which her grandmother, instead of giving Mary her usual bottle, produces a spoon (having now her chance to win the battle with her daughter-in-law over the timing of weaning), and: 'she thrusts something hard and metallic at my mouth, hurting my lips … a glutinous mess fills my mouth. I can't breathe. I am choking …'.

Then at bedtime: 'Where is my mummy? It is her nature to come back. She will come back, mummys always do. I know she is coming. I know. I know. I am frightened that what I know is not what is actually happening. Where is she? If she doesn't come where will I be? *Who* will I be? I cry helplessly. My grandmother relentlessly handles me with an unfamiliar touch, intrusive and unsympathetic.'

As day follows day, 'My protests at my mummy's absence are slipping me over an edge into despair … There is a terrible emptiness. I am dying … I am going to give up. I am powerless to bring her back by protesting. I thought that if I got really distressed, the distress would make her come. She hasn't come. I am empty inside, and around me everything is emptied out. There are the voices, the strangers, the terrible and violent intrusions with the metal and the slimy stuff … Most of all I want my mummy, who is now fading away, merging into the empty greyness of my world … I am in despair, despair which is pierced only by a terrible grief'.

When her parents eventually take her to the new house, they leave her crying in a strange room lest she should think she can control them into coming: 'My cries become screams. She still doesn't come. I wave my arms around, and my little hands emerging from the frilly sleeves are visually imprinted for ever on my memory.'

Mary successively inhabited children from many phases of her childhood, each burdened with the responsibility for, and care of, those inner children that preceded them.

It was this ability to inhabit parts of her self so completely that intensified the pain she felt when her earlier experiences were replicated in the transference situation, especially around any break in therapy. This was no less than agonising. There were times that I found it almost hard to believe in the sheer intensity of her pain. Was this a hysterical display, an attempt to invade and control me through a vengeful projective iden-tification? No doubt that element was present, but it was not predominant. Time and again I was brought back by her mani-fest truthfulness to a conviction of the immediate reality of her suffering. It was not a matter of her having been more hurt by her parents than many others: it was a capacity for suffering brought about by her dogged refusal to evade the childhood terror and pain. She allowed herself (or rather had to allow) the full agony of the baby, or in her words: 'the rage, hate, envy of a child cheated of meaning'. In Bion's words, she did indeed truly suffer her pain, as opposed to simply feeling it.

The resulting long-suppressed hatred found vent during one of the almost unendurable breaks in therapy:

Murder

I want to murder you,
Dorothy,
to eviscerate you
and leave your guts splattered all over your dusky pink carpet.

I want to murder you
and serve up your heart en cocotte
to your intimates
on your wrought iron garden table,
with your blood dripping
onto your Calder paving stones.

The poem continues with further ingenious images of torment, and ends:

I want you to suffer
the abandonment and the loss,
the rage and the terror,
the invalidity and the agony
that I have suffered.
And then, Dorothy,
I want you to tell me
That you understand.

It was long before Mary's poems began to speak of the reconciliations we were slowly winning through to. But gradually, her expressions of rage began to feel potentially empowering rather than incapacitating:

Anger

Anger severs the bonds between victim
and oppressor, snaps it like a dry twig.
. . .

Anger's a white bird swooping, laser-eyed,
into still worlds beneath white waves.

Anger's the spirit of life, moving swift
on the face of seething, raging waters;
...
             Anger connects
wounds to the soul's spark, and victims are freed
through the traitor's gate by which they came in.

Likewise, the grief that followed the anger, as depressive feelings
took hold:

Wells of tears

There are wells of tears
where the silence echoes
and the stone walls
are cool and strong;
             let me draw tears of grief
             only to receive back
             my lost self.
...
Wells of tears
are unblocked by the love of one who knows
how death seeps into the gaps
cracked open by separation;
             let me draw tears of terror
             that anoint my soul,
             pouring over me
             the gift of mourning;

             let me draw tears of loss
             that fill my emptiness
             with a new presence,
             a new place of meeting.

Then came a poem that signalled real change:

Loss

Knowing loss, we stare momentarily
into the abyss, only then to find
it also is transient, scuppering

our vague self-destructive plans to mud-slide
down its virtual slopes. And dawn breaking
over blank acres lights a racing sky.
Remember, the winds themselves are stateless;
in exile, see! - the whole world is our home.

Of the many passages in the therapy that contributed to change, I shall single out just one. That was when I found myself suddenly imagining her little brother sitting on an empty chair in our room, and decided to share it with her. It had a powerful effect: he acquired a reality for her not felt before. As a result, she went to find his grave, and placed beside it one of two stones taken from the place where their mother's ashes were scattered, keeping the other herself. This recognition that her brother was also her parents' child let him into a family relationship that before had seemed to belong only to her before. It created the sense of a bond with him, and allowed her to mourn the loss of a sibling, perhaps even a potential ally.

It was those poems that spoke of her experience of therapy that were the most expressive of the beauty of the method itself:

Psychotherapy

Dare to enter the cave while the tide
Is turned back – there are no bolts to bar the way.
Only wrench open the door that shuts out
understanding, and allow meaning
to flood the slime-coated caverns of the mind.

Here in the silence the sprit waits bright-eyed
like a white bird taut in the cleft of a rock
for the returning tide. Be still, as she sweeps
like a wind over the rushing water,
and as self pours in, enter the mystery.

To Dorothy, in her absence

        ... my Self
yearns to rise green from the black, trampled earth
and to reach for your open hands, waiting
patiently to part the very fibres
of my being, whilst I consent to know

loss, grief, desire, fear, and to undergo
rebirth into the safety of your gaze.

To Dorothy: about my teenager

My teenager is confused, not knowing
whether to present us both a bunch
of sarcastic apologies for her
very existence, give you a bouquet
for your skill and care as a therapist
or wilt into her gawky ugliness.
She longs to be loved into life, taken
into understanding arms and just held.
So be for me my sage midwife, bringing
by your gaze the mother in me to birth,
fiercely drawing, out of the barrenness
of the frozen wastes of my being, love
for my only child. Look at me; mirror
to me the image of me as mother.

And in a different vein:

To my absent therapist

I fear my healing process has lost its right direction
because my aching longing's evoked by your defection;
so individuation has got a poor prognosis,
since now my heart's desire is endless symbiosis.

It is of importance for my theme that looking back through
Mary's writings, one can see the moments when beauty struck
through the darkness to give her a sense of hope. At the age of
about twelve, on a family holiday in Scotland:

> I have in some sense found a home. The landscape speaks to
> me at a level which evokes a spiritual response through which
> I can transcend myself and all my worries and fears. Over
> the next few years, I fantasise endlessly about life in Scotland
> among the hills and the heather. A huge split is forming in
> me between my conflicts and my spiritual dimension which
> can potentially energise me to come home to myself'.

Then when she was older, watching from a train:

A vivid rainbow illuminates the Northumberland sky … [it] stirs some recognition in me. I know that 'everything will be all right' … There is somewhere within me a place where I am free of my father's possessive pressure.

And at a time of acute mental pain, suddenly:

An image comes into my mind of a lake surrounded by hills, the colours of a clear sky reflected in the absolute stillness of the water. A feeling of peace engulfs me. I begin to sense that there are other shores which I may be able to reach.

As we drew to the end of the therapy, she wrote this poem:

Dance of the spirit

I am poised on the threshold
of new life and freedom -
come, flaming spirit,
consume my fear,

seize me, and whirl me
into the bright vortex
of the dance;
teach me new steps;

excite me with your rhythms;
delight me with your laughter;
exhilarate me with the pattern
of your colourful choreography;

and in the pauses,
when music melts into silence,
draw me tenderly to rest
at the still centre
of the dance.

Most therapists would, no doubt, be able to identify patients who have especially enabled them to experience the beauty of the method. Mary stands out for me in this respect, and when I ask myself why, it seems to me that she was a person who had largely devoted herself to the pursuit of truth in various forms throughout her life (Mary began therapy in her mid-fifties) and was therefore unprepared to defend herself against the onslaught of truth when it manifested in reference to herself. Hence the inability to avoid the suffering that came in all the rawness of the child's hitherto unaddressed pain.

The decision(s) of one person to pursue truth – as Bion would say, to develop the K link – where another does not, is a mysterious one. I have not found myself able to explain it easily in terms of my patients' childhood experiences. For whatever reason, Mary was a person who took the promptings of her spiritual life unusually seriously; it would be difficult to point to any obvious cause for this in her background. It seems that Freud's mystery surrounding beauty (and therefore truth, in the sense understood in this book) remains unexplained, certainly as far as the longing for it is concerned. All I can say is that my abiding memory of Mary's therapy is of the way in which her beauty of expression mirrored the beauty of the inner process of obedience to the leadings of psychoanalytic truth.

Mary, talking about the then current news of a round-the-world yachtswoman, found tears coming to her eyes. She said, 'Because I'm crying, I know how powerful this metaphor is for me'. This way of putting it brought out Bion's sequencing: the bodily/emotional experience of the tears was followed by the thought that recognised their meaning. The metaphor was of Mary's own journey through therapy – a long and hard one, with water and coast as constant themes, often present in her poetry.

Here is a symbolic image with a clear significance. The yachtswoman's journey provides a fitting analogy for the emotional traveller: the encounter with wide and deep waters, the liminality of coastlines, loneliness, daring and adventure. Clearly too it is an example of, or akin to, Langer's 'art symbol', full of possibilities for further elaboration. So far, so satisfactory for the therapist and patient now in possession of a new and interesting piece of narrative. Yet such a definite symbolic 'steer' is in my experience unusual. Symbols, and the meanings behind them, are not often so readily identified; and in any event spring from underlying depths of symbolic thinking that remain largely unconscious.

To what deeper levels might Mary's metaphor also refer? This was not known to us from the metaphor itself, and not likely to be. Symbolic significance is more often recognised for its *sense* of meaning than for anything readily identifiable. David felt such a sense, along with experiences of awe and beauty, when in a deep gorge, or looking upward at a high mountain. The experience of being below something very great above him was profound, and he knew it was 'symbolic of something' – that the feelings it evoked contained something beyond and more than themselves. He did not know why, and that was not particularly important for him – the feeling, or knowledge, was enough, and always had the power to move him. The obvious possibilities of connecting this symbolic experience with being small and looking upward as a child did not seem relevant. Deliberately to scan a symbol with the conscious mind in search of a 'meaning' risks bypassing its true significance, or indeed laying false tracks over it that obscure rather than reveal. Sian Ellis, in her afore-mentioned essay, notes that 'Jung warned against analysing the life out of the symbol, "like the slain creature of the wild that can no longer run away"' (2017, p. 310).

As it is with the inaccessible regions of the individual mind, so with those of the human race as a whole. The ancient cave paintings and rock art found throughout the world, millennia old, provide tantalising half-insights into the early human mind. For the most part, these images carry the unmistakeable stamp of beauty, and brim with meaning. The meanings themselves we can do no more than speculate about, but what they do tell us beyond doubt is that the minds that created them understood symbol-making. The capacity to recognise emotional significance in mental imagery, to reinvest it with further significance, and to give aesthetic expression to the internal wealth thus created, has been with us far back into prehistoric time.

The American psychoanalyst Harold Blum, in his study of Eurasian cave painting: 'The psychological birth of art: A psychoanalytic approach to prehistoric cave art' (2011), explores the symbolism, consciously or unconsciously known, of the setting in which the art was created – the caves themselves. He imagines their dark interiors and long tunnels as symbolising the womb and birth passage. The awe and mystery surrounding these things are perhaps a reason for the caves having been kept for the art itself – he calls them 'the first art galleries' – since they appear to have been otherwise uninhabited. More than that, the paintings are in most instances hard to access, sited deep in the caves, so that even with today's equipment they can be very hard to reach. In these fastnesses the cave artist could be identified with 'the life-creating pregnant female in the womb of mother earth' (p. 199), creating life-like enduring images defending against transience and death.

A particularly striking insight is that of the cave being experienced as a transitional space. Here the art could be expressive of communication between inner and outer space, self and other. This is 'a dialogue that began with mother-infant sensory and affect-motor exchanges', a space

> for the emergence of self and object boundaries (Winnicott, 1957), the primal cavity (Spitz, 1965), the container for progressive parental transformation of the infant's affects and cognition (Bion, 1970), and the development of intrapsychic, interrelated self and object representations (Jacobson, 1964). (Blum, 2011, p. 199)

Again, the cave could 'unconsciously represent the head, the cranial cavity behind the eyes where imagery was likely located'. Using this imagery, the artists 'projected their attitudes and feelings onto or into the animals on the wall, imbued with human qualities' (p. 200), like the symbolic animals in children's stories. Considering their 'superlative' artistry, Blum concludes: 'The arrival of *Homo sapiens* about 40,000 – 50,000 years ago coincides with the birth of art ... The human creation of the arts is an intrinsic, universal propensity of human nature' (p. 202).

Some of the most movingly beautiful painting is found in the Dordogne region of France. Anyone who has seen the glorious rushing dance of the animals of Lascaux will surely testify not only to their astonishing beauty, but also to the intense purpose and meaning the artist conveys through them. Animal upon marvellous animal is joined in surging intention. What we see seems incredible – there is a mastery of line, colour, life and movement that carries with it a powerful emotional charge, calling out a correspondingly strong response in the viewer.

There are many interpretations of the origins and meanings of cave art, but it is interesting to note that Blum's psycho-analytic interpretation, with its insights into the underlying human psyche, need not deny or detract from any of them. This would include what is now accepted as perhaps the most likely explanation, that the paintings are the work of the shamanistic practitioner and healer. This places the caves as sacred spaces, imbued with symbolism by the human mind; and like the mind also in that there are likely to be countless paintings still hidden, probably never to be seen, especially in view of the diffi-culty of accessing them. Hence the cave scenario may be seen as symbolic of the symbol itself, its meaning sometimes clear, more often reaching back into impenetrable depths. For our purposes here, we can agree that such meanings, together with amazing beauty, are two central attributes that were undoubt-edly present in our remote ancestry.

Since Lascaux, humankind has taken forward its aesthetic inheritance into a myriad expressions of beauty. Turning now from our phylogenetic beginnings – the infancy, so to speak, of the race – I take from amongst these expressions a single paradigm, that of the infancy of the individual. Artists in all fields have throughout history offered their interpretations of the mother-baby gaze within the maternal reverie. This para-digm may be said to have underlain my theme, and it seems fitting to end with a few examples.

Religious depictions have figured largely, the Madonna-child a familiar theme of great paintings and of iconography. In many, the 'gaze' is symbolically rather than realistically portrayed, with Christ and Mary gazing outward, though clearly bonded together. One beautiful exception is that by Lippo Di Dalmasio's fourteenth century depiction of 'The Madonna of Humility', showing an exquisitely tender mutuality as mother and child gaze into one another's eyes. The spirit of these portrayals has been succinctly expressed by Angelo Scola as he sets out Von Balthasar's vision – a vision that brings powerfully to mind Meltzer's mother-baby scenario, imbued with the spirit of all-in-one circumincession. Scola speaks of:

> Balthasar's well-known description of approach to God by way of the I–Thou relation. It begins with the wondering gaze with which the baby perceives the smile on the loving countenance of its mother and learns that being, the whole of being, which is shining luminously for him on that face (*pulchrum*) is self-communicating love (*bonum*), and, in this self-communication, speaks and reveals itself (*verum*). (Scola, 1995, p. 7)

William Blake finely portrays the father-child relationship in his drawing 'Christ in the Carpenter's Shop'. Here Joseph's gaze is turned with loving intensity upon his son as he leans toward him, his saw forgotten in his hand. His whole bodily posture and expression reflect a pure and solemn absorption in the son who trustingly returns his gaze.

Turning to poetry, we have Wordsworth's famous passage from *The Prelude* beginning 'Bless'd the infant Babe' (II: 239–282). It is hard to paraphrase this, or to quote selectively, when the whole piece almost uncannily anticipates the combined insights of Bion and Meltzer into the baby's mind. Some key wording: 'Nurs'd in his Mother's arms ... [he]/ Doth gather passion from his Mother's eye!' Hence his mind becomes 'prompt and watchful', so that

> day by day,
> Subjected to the discipline of love,
> His organs and recipient faculties
> Are quicken'd, are more vigorous, his mind spreads,
> Tenacious of the forms which it receives.
> In one beloved presence ...

From that presence he derives 'a virtue which irradiates and exalts / All objects through all intercourse of sense', and:

> From nature largely he receives; nor so
> Is satisfied, but largely gives again,
> For feeling has to him imparted strength,
> And powerful in all sentiments of grief,
> Of exultation, fear, and joy, his mind,

>   Even as an agent of the one great mind,
>   Creates, creator and receiver both ...

This is 'the first Poetic spirit of our human life'.

The 'poetic spirit' of the baby's first encounter with the world is the inheritance of all of us who are privileged to work in the later close encounters with our patients and clients. Wordsworth's poetry combines beauty and insight in a way we may all hope to do as we engage in Meltzer's 'most interesting conversation in the world'.

So, in the night of day
    rarely, rarely,
    beauty
    startles;
    and we obey.

(R. J. Harris, from 'Night Phone'
    in *A Journey Abroad*, 2018)

REFERENCES

Allen, D. W. (1974). *The Fear of Looking.* Charlottesville, VA: University Press of Virginia.

Bacon, F. ([1625] 1985). Of beauty. In: *Essays.* London: Penguin.

Balthasar, H. U. von (1989). *The Glory of the Lord: A Theological Aesthetics,* ed. J . Fessio & J. Riches. Edinburgh: T & T Clark.

Bernstein, J. (1973). *Einstein.* New York: Viking Press.

Bettelheim, B. (1982). *Freud and Man's Soul.* Vintage Books, 1984.

Bion, W.R. (1965). *Transformations.* London: Heinemann.

Bion, W.R. (1967) *Second Thoughts.* Karnac.

Bion, W. R. (1970). *Attention and Interpretation.* London. Tavistock Publications.

Bion, W.R. (1973–1974). *Brazilian Lectures.* 2 vols. Rio de Janeiro; Imago.

Bion, W. R. (1980). Bion in New York and San Paolo. Perthshire: Clunie Press.

Bion, W.R. (1987). *Clinical Seminars and Four Papers,* ed. F. Bion. Abingdon: Fleetwood Press.

Bion, W.R. (1991). A *Memoir of the Future.* 3 volume edition. London: Karnac.

Bion, W. R. (1997). *Taming Wild Thoughts,* ed. F. Bion. London: Karnac.

Blum, H. P. (2011). The psychological birth of art: a psychoanalytic approach to prehistoric cave art. *International Forum of Psychoanalysis,* 20: 196–204.

Bollas, C. (1987). *The Shadow of the Object: Psychoanalysis of the Unthought Known.* Columbia University Press.

Botbol Acreche, M. (2000). Daily beauty and daily ugliness. *Intercambios* (digital papers on psychoanalysis), (4), 7–17.

Brady, E. (2003). *Aesthetics of the Natural Environment,* Edinburgh University Press.

Carlson, A., & Berleant, A. (Eds.). (2004). *The Aesthetics of Natural Environments.* Toronto: Broadview Press.

Chasseguet-Smirgel, J. (1985). *The Ego Ideal: A Psychoanalytic Essay on the Malady of the Ideal.* London: Free Association Books.

Cohen, M. & Hahn, A (Eds). (2000). *Exploring the Work of Donald Meltzer: A Festschrift.* London: Karnac.

Cox, M. & Theilgaard, A. (1987). *Mutative Metaphors in Psychotherapy: The Aeolian Mode.* London: Tavistock.

Croce, B. ([1909] 1967). *Aesthetic.* London: Vision Press.

Danto, A. C. (2003). *The Abuse of Beauty: Aesthetics and the Concept of Art.* Chicago: Open Court.

Dietrich, E. (2015). *Excellent Beauty.* Cambridge University Press.

Ellis, S. (2017). Apprehending the translucent in the art of supervision. *British Journal of Psychotherapy,* 33(3), 297–311.

Euripides (2001). *The Bacchae.* Harvard Classics, vol. 8. New York: Bartleby.

Freud, S. (1916). On transience. *SE,* 14: 303–307.

Freud, S. (1930). *Civilization and its Discontents. SE,* 21: 57–146.

Glover, N. (2009). *Psychoanalytic Aesthetics: An Introduction to the British School.* London: Harris Meltzer Trust.

Gosline, A. (2004). Babies prefer to gaze upon beautiful faces. *New Scientist,* 6 September.

Grotstein, J. (2007). *A Beam of Intense Darkness: Wilfred Bion's Legacy to Psychoanalysis.* London: Karnac.

Hagman, G. (2005). *Aesthetic Experience: Beauty, Creativity and the Search for the Ideal.* Amsterdam: Rodopi.

Harris, R. J. (2018). *A Journey Abroad: Wartime Poems Serving with the FAU,* ed. M. H. Williams. London: Harris Meltzer Trust.

Hepburn, R. (1966). Contemporary Aesthetics and the Neglect of Natural Beauty. In: Williams, B., and Montefiore, A. (Eds.), *British*

Analytical Philosophy, pp. 285–310. London: Routledge.

Hepburn, R. (2004). Landscape and the metaphysical imagination. In: Carlson, A., & Berleant, A. (Eds.). *The Aesthetics of Natural Environments*, pp. 127–140. Toronto: Broadview Press.

Hillman, J. (1998). The practice of beauty. In: Beckley, B., & Shapiro, D. (Eds.), *Uncontrollable Beauty: Towards a New Aesthetics*, pp. 261–274. New York: Allworth Press.

House, F. (2001). The face of the therapist in psychotherapy practice. *Journal of the British Association of Psychotherapists*, 39: 30–45.

Huxley, T. H. (1894). Evolution and Ethics. In: *Collected Essays*, vol. 9, pp. 46–116.

Kant, I. (1987). *Critique of Pure Reason*. Transl. W. Pluhar. Indianapolis: Hackett.

Kirwan, J. (1999). *Beauty.* Manchester University Press.

Kuspit, D. (2002). Beauty matters. *Artnet Magazine*, 23(7).

Jefferies, R. (1909). *The Hills and the Vale*. Oxford University Press.

Jung, C. (1931). *The Spirit in Man, Art and Literature. CW*, 15. London: Routledge.

Jung, C. (1960). *The Symbolic Life. CW*, 18. London: Routledge.

Langlois, J. H., et al. (1987). Infant preferences for attractive faces: rudiments of a stereotype? *Developmental Psychology*, 23 (3): 363–369.

Likierman, M. (1989). The clinical significance of aesthetic experience. *International Review of Psychoanalysis*, 16: 133–150.

Maizels, N. (2009). Foreword. In: Glover, N., *Psychoanalytic Aesthetics*. London: Harris Meltzer Trust.

Meltzer, D. (1967). *The Psychoanalytical Process*. London: Heinemann.

Meltzer, D. (1973). On the apprehension of beauty. *Contemporary Psychoanalysis*, 9 (2): 224–229.

Meltzer, D., et al. (1975). *Explorations in Autism*. Perthshire: Clunie Press.

Meltzer, D. ([1976] 1994). Temperature and distance as technical dimensions of interpretation. In: *Sincerity: Collected Papers of Donald Meltzer*, ed. A. Hahn, pp. 374–386. London: Karnac.

Meltzer, D. (1978). *The Kleinian Development*. 3 vols. Perthshire: Clunie Press.

Meltzer, D. ([1986] 2018). *Studies in Extended Metapsychology.* Perthshire: Clunie Press.

Meltzer, D. (1987). On aesthetic reciprocity. *Journal of Child*

Psychotherapy, 13 (2), 3–14.

Meltzer, D., & Williams, M. H. (1988). T*he Apprehension of Beauty: The Role of Aesthetic Conflict in Development, Art and Violence.* Perthshire: Clunie Press.

Milner, M. (1952). Aspects of symbolism in comprehension of the not-self. *The International Journal of Psychoanalysis,* 33: 181–195.

Milner, M. (1969). *The Hands of the Living God: An Account of a Psychoanalytic Treatment.* London: Routledge.

Milner, M. (1987a). *Eternity's Sunrise: A Way of Keeping a Diary.* London: Routledge.

Milner, M. (1987b). *The Suppressed Madness of Sane Men.* London: Tavistock.

Murray, W. H. ([1947] 1992). *Mountaineering in Scotland.* Sheffield: Baton Wicks.

Negri, R. (1994). T*he Newborn in the Intensive Care Unit.* Perthshire: Clunie Press.

Orwell, G. (1935). *A Clergyman's Daughter.* Penguin Books Ltd, 1979.

Pearson, J. (Ed.) (2004). *Analyst of the Imagination: The Life and Work of Charles Rycroft.* London: Karnac.

Pistiner de Cortinas, L. (2009). *The Aesthetic Dimension of the Mind: Variations on a Theme of Bion.* London: Routledge.

Plato. (1952). T*he Symposium.* Penguin Classics.

Plato. (2005). *Phaedrus.* Digireads.com Publishing.

Poincaré, H. (1952). *Science and Method.* Transl. F. Maitland. Cornell University Press.

Pistiner de Cortiñas, L. (2009). *The Aesthetic Dimension of the Mind: Variations on a Theme of Bion.* London: Karnac.

Rodin, A. ([1911] 1958). On Art and Artists. London: Peter Owen.

Rycroft, C. (1979). *The Innocence of Dreams.* London: Hogarth Press.

Rycroft, C. (1985). *Psychoanalysis and Beyond.* London: Hogarth Press.

Rycroft, C. (2018). *Imagination and Reality: Psychoanalytical Essays 1951–1961.* London: Routledge.

Segal. H. (1952). A psychoanalytical approach to aesthetics. *International Journal of Psychoanalysis,* 33: 196–207.

Scola, A. (1995). *Hans Urs von Balthasar: A Theological Style.* Grand Rapids: Eerdmans. 1995.

Slater, A., et al. (2000). The role of facial orientation in newborn infants' preference for attractive faces. *Developmental Science,* 3 (2): 181–185.

Turner, J. (2002). A brief history of illusion: Milner, Winnicott, Rycroft.

International Journey of Psychoanalysis, 83: 1063–1082.

Whitehead, A. N. ([1929] 2010). *Process and Reality.* Simon and Schuster.

Williams, G. P. (2000). Reflections on 'aesthetic reciprocity'. In: Cohen, M., & Hahn, A. (Eds.), *Exploring the Work of Donald Meltzer: A Festschrift.* London: Karnac.

Williams, M. (1922 [1995]). *The Velveteen Rabbit, or How Toys Become Real.* London: Puffin Books.

Williams, M. H. (2005). *The Vale of Soulmaking: The Post-Kleinian Model of the Mind.* London: Routledge.

Williams, M. H. (2010). *The Aesthetic Development: The Poetic Spirit of Psychoanalysis: Essays on Bion, Meltzer, Keats.* London: Routledge.

Williams, M. H. (Ed.). (2018). *Aesthetic Conflict and its Clinical Relevance.* London: Harris Meltzer Trust.

Winnicott, D. W. (1971). *Playing and Reality.* London: Tavistock.

Winnicott, D. W. (1974). Fear of breakdown. *International Review of Psychoanalysis,* 1: 103–7.

Wright, K. (1991). *Vision and Separation: Between Mother and Baby.* New York: Aronson.

Wurmser, L. (1981). *The Mask of Shame.* Johns Hopkins University Press.

NAME INDEX